MW00676057

Strategic Studies Institute
and
U.S. Army War College Press

A HISTORY OF THE U.S. ARMY OFFICER CORPS, 1900-1990

Arthur T. Coumbe

September 2014

*****

Comments pertaining to this report are invited and should be forwarded to: Director, Strategic Studies Institute and U.S. Army War College Press, U.S. Army War College, 47 Ashburn Drive, Carlisle, PA 17013-5010.

*****

All Strategic Studies Institute (SSI) and U.S. Army War College (USAWC) Press publications may be downloaded free of charge from the SSI website. Hard copies of this report may also be obtained free of charge while supplies last by placing an order on the SSI website. SSI publications may be quoted or reprinted in part or in full with permission and appropriate credit given to the U.S. Army Strategic Studies Institute and U.S. Army War College Press, U.S. Army War College, Carlisle, PA. Contact SSI by visiting our website at the following address: *www.StrategicStudiesInstitute.army.mil.*

*****

The Strategic Studies Institute and U.S. Army War College Press publishes a monthly email newsletter to update the national security community on the research of our analysts, recent and forthcoming publications, and upcoming conferences sponsored by the Institute. Each newsletter also provides a strategic commentary by one of our research analysts. If you are interested in receiving this newsletter, please subscribe on the SSI website at *www.StrategicStudiesInstitute.army.mil/newsletter.*

ISBN 1-58487-637-9

CONTENTS

FOREWORD

The Army's Office of Economic and Manpower Analysis published a series of monographs that were intended to provide a theoretical and conceptual framework for the development of an Army Officer Corps Strategy. These monographs consider the creation and maintenance of a highly skilled Officer Corps in the context of the nation's continuing commitment to an all-volunteer military, its far flung international interests, and ongoing changes in its domestic labor market. The authors contend that the confluence of these factors demands a comprehensive Officer Corps strategy recognizing the interdependency of accessing, developing, retaining, and employing talent. In their view, building a talent-focused strategy around this four-activity human capital model would best posture the Army to match individual officer competencies to specific competency requirements.

To provide historical context to these monographs, Dr. Arthur Coumbe of the Office of Economic and Manpower Analysis has prepared a monograph that provides a historical overview of the Army Officer Corps and its management in the modern era. Like the earlier monographs, this volume is organized around what the Office of Economic and Manpower Analysis sees as the functionally interdependent concepts of accessing, developing, retaining, and employing talent.

The chapters in this book will take the reader up to the point where the earlier monographs begin their story in the late-1980s.

Douglas C. Lovelace, Jr.

DOUGLAS C. LOVELACE, JR.
Director
Strategic Studies Institute and
    U.S. Army War College Press

ABOUT THE AUTHOR

ARTHUR T. COUMBE is a historian with the Army's Office of Economic and Manpower Analysis and an adjunct faculty member at American Military University. A retired Army officer, he has authored a number of articles and books on Army ROTC history and the Franco-Prussian War of 1870-71. Dr. Coumbe received a B.S from the U.S. Military Academy and a Ph.D. from Duke University.

SUMMARY

With the assistance of the Strategic Studies Institute of the U.S. Army War College, the Army's Office of Economic and Manpower Analysis published a series of monographs that were intended to provide a theoretical and conceptual framework for the development of an Army Officer Corps Strategy. These monographs consider the creation and maintenance of a highly skilled Officer Corps in the context of the nation's continuing commitment to an all-volunteer military, its far flung international interests, and ongoing changes in its domestic labor market. The authors of the various monographs believe that the confluence of these factors demands a comprehensive Officer Corps strategy that recognizes the interdependency of accessing, developing, retaining, and employing talent. In their view, building a talent-focused strategy around this four-activity human capital model would best enable the Army to match individual officer competencies to specific competency requirements.

Dr. Arthur Coumbe of the Office of Economic and Manpower Analysis has prepared a monograph that provides a historical overview of the Army Officer Corps and its management in the modern era. Like the earlier monographs, this volume is organized around what the Office of Economic and Manpower analysis see as the functionally interdependent concepts of accessing, developing, retaining, and employing talent. This book is a prologue to the earlier monographs that begin their story in the late-1980s.

CHAPTER 1

OVERVIEW

INTRODUCTION

The Army has never had an overarching and inte-grative plan to **access, develop, retain**, and **employ** its officers through a career of service. In the past, it has addressed one or another of these facets of an officer strategy but always in a desultory and piecemeal fash-ion. Recently, the Army's senior leaders have begun to formulate such a strategy based on the principle of talent management, although this effort is still in its infancy and still has not gained the assent of all concerned parties. Indeed, many senior leaders doubt both its feasibility and its desirability.

The basic outline of this talent-based officer strat-egy was adumbrated in a series of monographs au-thored by Casey Wardynski, David Lyle, and Mike Colarusso of the G-1's Office of Economic and Man-power Analysis (OEMA) and published by the Strate-gic Studies Institute in 2009 and 2010.[1]

The purpose of the present volume is to supple-ment these OEMA monographs by providing a histor-ical context for their discussion of an officer strategy. First is offered an overview of some key developments and assumptions that have guided and shaped the Of-ficer Corps and the way it has been managed over the last century. It is meant as a companion piece for *To-ward an Officer Corps Strategy: A Talent Focused Human Capital Model*. By design, I have sacrificed nuance for clarity as I attempt to highlight general trends.

THE ROOT REFORMS

The U.S. Army Officer Corps, along with the policies and assumptions that underpin its management, has passed through several watersheds since the turn of the 20th century. The first began during the tenure of corporation lawyer, Elihu Root, as Secretary of War (1899-1903).

Root's stint in the War Department took place in an era when industry was eclipsing agriculture as the nation's predominant economic sector, when the railroad and modern means of communication were lacing the country together economically, and when an assertive progressivism was conditioning the public to expect more out of their government. Perhaps this socioeconomic setting partially explains why the transformation effected under Root was very different than previous ones experienced by the Army. The latter were largely unplanned affairs, driven by the force of circumstances and individual initiative, while the former was centrally directed and institutionally driven.[2]

Under Root's tutelage, the Army began its transformation from a constabulary force focused on policing the frontier to an "Army for Empire," concerned with hemispheric defense and burdened with wide-ranging imperial responsibilities. The key event for Root and his supporters within the War Department was the Spanish American War. That conflict and its consequences precipitated a substantial increase in troop strength. The Army grew from a force of about 27,000 men with 2,000 officers in the 1890s to a force of 90,000 men and 4,000 officers by 1913.[3]

The conflict with Spain also inspired an extensive military reorganization. In the aftermath of the war, Root and his allies in the War Department recognized the need for the Army to remold itself into an institution capable of managing its newly acquired global responsibilities. Those new responsibilities entailed the overseas stationing of units and leaders. Over the next decade, the Army established and garrisoned a series of outposts and bases stretching from the Caribbean to the Far East.

Its extended global and functional reach required the Army to shed the antiquated bureau system, which had guided military administration since the late-18th century, and adopt of a system of integrated management. Accordingly, Root moved to displace the quasi-independent and powerful bureau chiefs with a Chief of Staff who answered to the Secretary of War. It was a long, tough, and rancorous fight, but the power of the bureau chiefs was greatly reduced, albeit not extinguished, by the time the United States emerged from World War I.[4]

A consolidation of units at fewer locations and the elimination of small, uneconomical posts was another aspect of Root's reform agenda. So was his attempt to gather a dispersed frontier constabulary into larger tactical units, a task continued by his successors, who eventually designed nominal divisional organizations to link these units together in an inchoate force structure. His effort to transform the Organized Militia, or what is now known as the National Guard (NG), into a tiered reserve and thereby realize John Calhoun's concept of an expansible Army was yet another part of his reform program. This latter task was accomplished principally through the Dick Act of 1903, which established a new and closer relationship between the

Regular Army (RA) and the NG. In a move that was to transform the way the Army developed its leaders, Root introduced a progressive and sequential system of professional military education designed to prepare officers for specific stages in their careers. The system encompassed garrison schools, branch schools, the staff college at Ft. Leavenworth, KS, and the newly created U.S. Army War College (USAWC).

The new arrangements sparked dramatic changes in officer management. In the place of the old system, in which promotions, assignments, and virtually everything else in an officer's career were regulated by the regiment, arose the prototype of the modern officer management system that featured a career pattern characterized by a rotation between staff and line assignments and was punctuated with periodic professional training. Root's was essentially an industrial age blueprint inspired by the Prussian military paradigm and reinforced by the corporate production model which, by Root's time, had become a prevalent form of business organization. Together, the organizational and educational overhaul of the Army under Root signaled the ultimate demise of the frontier Army and the regimental system that sustained it.

A milestone of sorts occurred in 1907 when the War Department replaced the policy of unit rotation with a policy of individual replacements to sustain the Army overseas. This change was significant and symbolic. It reflected not only the weakening of the regimental system but the Army's expanding size and responsibilities and its new and increasing emphasis on modern management practices and the commitment to industrial efficiency that they necessarily entailed.[5]

WORLD WAR I

The outbreak of war in Europe in 1914 occasioned a refinement of Root's paradigm. On the eve of that conflict, the Army was capable of fulfilling its imperial responsibilities, prosecuting conflicts on the scale of the Spanish American War and orchestrating deployments on the volatile Mexican border. It was not, however, equipped or configured for a mass mobilization. Root had been impressed with the ideas of Emory Upton and his like-minded contemporaries who were chary of growth beyond the organizational bounds of established units. Controllable numbers of raw recruits could be trained to a high standard by professional officers and noncommissioned officers (NCOs) in such units while routine operations continued under veteran troops. Such an **expansible** force could double in size in a relatively short period without sacrificing its quality. Adherence to the concept of an expansible Army was therefore a commitment to modest and measured growth.

Given the geographical isolation of the United States, the insular character of its overseas territories, and the relative weakness of its neighbors to the north and south, this seemed adequate, even with an RA of fewer than 100,000 men. Many American professional Soldiers admired the elaborate mass mobilization models of the major European powers but considered these models inappropriate for or irrelevant to their own military.[6]

But in 1914, conditions began to change. As the European War dragged on, public concern about preparedness mounted. The United States took its first rather tentative steps toward the ideal of the Nation in Arms when the Congress passed the National Defense

Act of 1916, which substantially augmented both the RA and the NG and rendered both further expansible along essentially Uptonian lines. The act introduced measures for industrial and economic mobilization and recognized the universal military obligation of the "unorganized Militia" under federal auspices. This latter measure laid the groundwork for mass conscription, followed by the organization and training of new divisions under the supervision of small cadres of professional soldiers. When America entered the war in April 1917, the system described in the National Defense Act of 1916 appeared as the only practicable way to field forces large enough and quickly enough to render meaningful assistance to the allies before it was too late. For the emergency, later known as World War I, the new "National Army" raised 18 divisions, joining eight constructed from the RA and 17 from the NG to defeat the Germans in Europe. In the process of organizing the American Expeditionary Force (AEF), divisions became solidified, and corps and armies were added to control them.[7]

World War I necessitated adjustments to the Army's officer accessions and management practices. Before that conflict, the Army obtained its officers from West Point, civil life, and, to a very limited degree, the enlisted ranks. Due to the immense scale of the war, the Army turned to Officer Training Schools (OTS), the progenitors of the modern Officer Candidate School (OCS) system, for the vast majority of its junior leaders for the combat arms while it used direct appointments from civil life to fill out the specialty branches (an arrangement which rendered mixed results). Although the first OTS classes (following the pre-war "Plattsburgh" formula) admitted substantial numbers of so-called social elites, the War Department soon evidenced a preference for enlisted men as officer aspirants for the arms. In this clash of massive, industrial era armies, the Army's most pressing need was **for technically proficient platoon leaders, not for broadly educated junior officers adept at sophisticated abstract reasoning and prepared for a career of military service**.

The Army's first foray into large scale officer management took place during this time. It was necessitated by the Officer Corps' rapid expansion from about 6,000 officers in April 1917 to over 200,000 officers by August 1918 and the War Department's imperative to "simplify the procedure of discovering [officer] talent and assigning it where most needed." Before the war, combat arms officers had been under the control of the Adjutant General, while permanent members of the specialist branches were under the control of their branch chiefs. However, during World War I, assignments and promotions for all officers were shifted to the General Staff. At the conclusion of the war, the Chief of Staff expressed the hope that the General Staff would eventually be empowered to:

> control the entering into the service of officers, their assignments, promotion, and separation from the service in such a way as to place and reward individuals more impartially to the best interests of the service, and to meet any emergency requiring an expansion of our military forces, in a manner that has not heretofore been possible.[8]

This hope was not fulfilled.

To better match its needs for talent with the available manpower, the War Department developed the Officer Qualification Card and the Commissioned Officers Rating Scale. Both devices were intended to match skills and attributes with leadership requirements.[9] Given the tremendous scope of the task, the vast needs of the AEF, and the suddenness with which the war was thrust on the Army, the system of matching talent to position did not function very efficiently, of course. Still, a start had been made, and the Army learned much that it would later use in the next world war.

INTERWAR YEARS

After the war, the U.S. Army shrank from its wartime high of almost 2.5 million men to about 140,000 while its officer strength declined from 130,000 to 12,000. In the demobilization, it abandoned wartime officer accessions and management systems and returned to its traditional methods. During the interwar years, one of the Army's main purposes was to provide training and leadership for a temporary mass citizen Army should the need for such a force arise. This mobilization-based mass Army was predicated on the notion that small cadres could train large units to appropriate standards within reasonable periods of time. Proponents of the citizen soldier military ideal, such as John McAuley Palmer, took the AEF as their model when the Army was reconstructed after the armistice. These observers viewed the RA not as an expansible core à la John Calhoun, but as a force capable of deploying on short notice. The NG, they reasoned, would take longer to mobilize but was a readily accessible reserve. Behind this glacis of early deploying units, a great mass of new divisions under small cadres of experienced officers and NCOs could organize, train, and deploy. This approach was solidified in the National Defense Act of 1920, although interwar frugality much diminished the preparedness of the RA and NG.[10]

The system of officer development schools introduced by Secretary Root remained in place, but it was gradually expanded and refined. The branch schools retained their vitality although, due to budgetary restrictions, the time that junior officers spent in them was slightly reduced. The U.S. Army Command and General Staff College (CGSC) at Ft. Leavenworth thrived, and attendance there became a mark of professional distinction and a virtual prerequisite for high rank. The USAWC retained an active role, both as an educational institution and as an agency to guide and sort through good ideas. In all schools, adjustments were made in curricula to incorporate the lessons learned in the war and the perceived demands of a new and somewhat uncertain international environment.[11]

Although vestiges of the bureau system remained, responsibility for long-range planning increasingly fell to the General Staff, which saw its scope expanded and its role become more specialized and refined. In 1921, the Army recognized the enhanced importance of the personnel management function by creating a Personnel Division of the General Staff. This move rationalized personnel management to a degree but did not break the power of the branch chiefs, whose control over their respective fiefdoms remained as strong as ever.

The chiefs of services, or branches as they are called today, retained their power throughout the interwar period. In fact, they had an importance rivaling that of the Chief of Staff himself. They were, according to General Bruce Palmer, "the Mama, Papa, [and] Mecca" for the RA officer, controlling virtually every aspect of his professional life.[12]

In the 1920s and 1930s, the Army's regular Officer Corps busied itself with planning for war, training troops, working with the reserve components, garrisoning overseas possessions, and providing for the support and sustenance of the force. The focus of most officers was on internal troop training and administration. The professional code that governed their lives emphasized ritual and rectitude, a faultless technique with weapons, and the maintenance of high standards of appearance. Less than 5 percent of the Officer Corps was engaged in any type of activity that took them away from daily troop problems.[13]

The insular character of the officer's existence began to erode in the mid-1930s as a result of an increasingly threatening international situation. At the very apex of the Army, senior officers became more concerned with international affairs, and a few began to turn their attention, along with that of their subordinates, to strategic matters. Lower down on the Army's functional pyramid, officers sought to broaden their technical training and professional education in the growing field of support functions—services of supply, finance, weapons technology, research and development, public relations, personnel management, and industrial mobilization. Still, it would take the shock of World War II to expand the focus of the Officer Corps as a whole beyond unit training and administration.[14]

The promotion prospects for officers were quite bleak throughout most of the interwar period. Following the armistice, the Army reduced many officers to their permanent RA grade and introduced a single promotion list to replace the old branch promotion system. Under this new system, there was no opportunity for the most capable officers to "jump files" and get promoted ahead of their less capable compatriots. Everything depended on seniority.

The famous "hump" was another impediment to promotion. After the war, thousands of officers commissioned during the emergency were retained to lead the interwar Army, which, despite its diminutive size, was still much larger that the pre-war force. By 1926, after several rather small adjustments were made in officer strength, there remained in an Officer Corps of 12,000, a total of 5,800 officers who had been commissioned between 1916 and 1918. Consequently, many officers spent most of their career in the same grade. It was not at all uncommon for an officer to remain a lieutenant for 17 years.[15] Only with the outbreak of World War II would promotion opportunities for regulars open up once again.[16]

By design, West Point, NY, was the principal source of regular officers during this era. Senior military colleges and, to a lesser extent, civilian universities, supplemented the output of the U.S. Military Academy (USMA), while the enlisted ranks were an insignificant source of new lieutenants. In peacetime, the War Department was not looking for immediately employable platoon leaders but **for junior officers with a broad inventory of intellectual skills and abilities that would make them valuable senior leaders in the Army of the future.**[17]

WORLD WAR II

The War Department entered the war with a number of RA and NG divisions in various states of readiness. To this core was, in the fashion of World War I, added new Army of the United States (AUS) divisions, with a ratio of only one regular Soldier for each conscript. These AUS divisions completed a 1-year training cycle before entering the deployment queue.

By the end of the war, conscripts composed the bulk of all divisions – RA, NG, and AUS – and meaningful distinctions between them evaporated. To the corps and army structure adopted in World War I, the War Department added the army group in World War II. The mobilization-based Army of the latter war needed a greatly expanded command hierarchy to direct it.[18]

World War II saw the Officer Corps grow from 14,000 to 835,000. To effect this expansion, the War Department decentralized officer management in 1942. It created three major commands – the Army Ground Forces (AGF), the Army Service Forces (ASF), and the Army Air Forces (AAF) – to control and administer the training and assignment of officers who fell within their functional purview. Many critics attributed the Army's officer management problems during the war to this decentralized system.

One of the most troubling issues with this system was the severe distributional imbalance that existed among the various branches. Throughout most of the war, there were far too many anti-aircraft and field artillery officers and too few infantry, armor, and engineer officers. This system was also blamed for officer "pooling." In 1943, the Army's Inspector General reported that about half of all ASF officers had been sitting in replacement pools for extended periods, where they attended "makeshift" training, intended primarily to keep them busy. It seemed that officers who lacked desired skills and ability were being shunted into these pools because they were not wanted in units. Reclassification of these marginal performers was not a viable option because of extremely cumbersome administrative procedures it involved.[19]

The vast majority of officers who led the Army of 8,300,000 men came from one of three sources: 1) from those who had received training in peacetime military agencies—the NG, the Officers' Reserve Corps (ORC), the Reserve Officers' Training Corps (ROTC), and the Citizens' Military Training Camps (CMTC); 2) from a body of civilians with special skills (who were awarded direct commissions); and 3) from OCS. OCS was by far the largest source of new officers. In its selection of OCS candidates, the Army favored enlisted men, since they were thought to make the best platoon leaders—superior to ROTC and even USMA graduates.

During the war, the existing educational facilities of the Army focused upon immediate requirements—i.e., training large numbers of men for specific duties in an emergency situation. In this environment, education was greatly curtailed. At West Point, courses were compressed and accelerated as they had been in World War I, albeit less drastically. Beginning in 1942, cadets were commissioned in 3 rather than 4 years. Army service schools saw their courses shortened or suspended. The USAWC was completely closed down.[20]

FROM WORLD WAR TO COLD WAR

After the war, the dynamics of national defense changed drastically as the United States gradually grew into its role as leader of the non-communist world. To fulfill the responsibilities that its new role entailed, it engineered the erection of a network of alliances whose collective reach stretched across the globe. At the same time, the nation effected a major reorganization of its defense establishment. The National Defense Act of 1947 restructured the nation's military forces into three services presided over by a department of defense. Strategy underwent a revolution, as nuclear weapons and the new international system that these weapons helped fashion began to drive both planning and force structure.[21]

In terms of its troop units, the trend was for the Army to morph into a constabulary force overseas while maintaining a large mobilization base in the continental United States (CONUS) in case it was called upon to fight a reprise of World War II. There were large variations in troop strength during this period. After shrinking from over 8,000,000 troops in August 1945 to less than 600,000 by June 1950, the Army expanded to more than 1.6 million men to fight the Korean war. After that war, it contracted moderately but remained large enough to fulfill the nation's containment strategy, elaborated in National Security Council (NSC)-68 and other documents. Except for a brief time in the late-1940s when it conducted an experiment with a volunteer force, the Army relied on conscription and individual replacements to man the force.

An elaborate and expandable mobilization structure emerged in the post-war era. After the active forces, the most readily and quickly deployable units were maintained in the NG and the Army Reserve (AR). In addition to its troop units, the AR maintained training divisions capable of raising completely new units on the order of the AUS divisions used in World War II.

The conscription-based Army of the early-Cold War featured high attrition rates, a condition that Army planners integrated into their policies and estimates. Careerists in that Army rapidly rotated through a variety of assignments; all were expected to take their fair share of "hardship" tours, accompanied overseas tours, tours in CONUS, and school assignments. Homesteading, i.e., staying at one post and in one unit for an extended period, was an unforgivable professional sin. A complex bureaucracy, focused more on plugging "faces into spaces" rather than on fitting the "right person to the right job," arose to control all these moves.

In this mobilization-centered Army, personnel managers developed sophisticated tools to induct, classify, distribute, and discharge the hundreds of thousands of short-term Soldiers who passed through the ranks. Standardized testing, which had been used intermittently since World War I, now became a staple of personnel management. Mental categories such as CAT IV assumed great symbolic as well as practical significance. Units and agencies found themselves struggling with one another for Soldiers with the preferred skills, knowledge, and attributes while personnelists classified, managed, and tracked the military workforce more closely than ever before.

World War II ended what one historian has referred to as the "golden age" of the branch chiefs. After the war, a "semi-centralized" career management division was set up to oversee officer assignments. Still, continuity was more evident than change. The branches remained powerful entities and continued to regulate career patterns.[22]

The old, interwar Army had been relatively uncomplicated, small, close-knit, and somewhat insular. The Army that emerged after World War II, however, was large, multifarious, somewhat disjointed, egalitarian, and more integrated into society as a whole. Whereas the interwar Officer Corps was intended to provide the nucleus for a temporary mass Army, the new one was called upon to lead a permanent standing Army capable of dealing with the global threat posed by the Soviet Union, while at the same time maintaining its capability for mass mobilization.[23]

The Army sought to achieve a wider distribution of talented officers to deal with the more complex and wide-ranging threat it faced in the post-war era. National security now entailed diplomacy, science, foreign aid, and industrial and technological development as much as it did traditional military training. Once again, the Army's system of officer development was refined and enlarged to incorporate the lessons of the last war and to meet the challenges posed by the new international order.[24]

After dominating the peacetime Officer Corps for a century and a half, West Point lost its quantitative preeminence as a commissioning source. The vast size of the U.S. Cold War defense establishment led to this loss of ascendancy. ROTC, which produced junior officers with a wide range of academic skills, became the engine of the Army's Officer Corps. By the mid-1950s, in fact, ROTC was producing twice as many regular officers as West Point and nearly 80 percent of the short-term Reserve officers who filled out the junior officer ranks. OCS was retained but drastically reduced in scope.[25]

Officer management was placed on a new footing with the passage of the Officer Personnel Act of 1947, which allowed for greater flexibility in the handling of officers. Prior to the passage of this legislation, it had been practically impossible to eliminate poor performers, which resulted in the Army being filled with hundreds, perhaps thousands, of colonels and lieutenant colonels it did not want. The Army published its first technical manual for officer career management in response to this legislation. In this manual, career management objectives were crafted to channel an officer's career into different types of jobs within the confines of his assigned branch. Extended or repetitive duty in any single capacity was to be avoided at all costs; like homesteading, specialization was a professional sin.[26] The basic objective of officer management remained "to develop a highly competent Officer Corps to serve in positions of progressively higher responsibility in the event of a national emergency." The end result of the process was to be a broadly trained officer, capable of grasping the wide sweep of the Army's missions and responsibilities.[27]

Many of the assumptions and policies that underpinned officer career management at this time were shared in the corporate world. Like the Army, corporations in the post-World War II era aimed to develop general management skills in prospective executives by encouraging lateral career moves across functions and departments. The end result, it was hoped, would be a leader capable of grasping the entirety of the corporation's operations.[28]

THE TURBULENT 1960s AND EARLY-1970s

The period encompassing the 1960s and the early-1970s witnessed the transformation of the conscript Army of the early-Cold War to the volunteer Army of the late-Cold War. It also saw the weakening, albeit not the extinction, of the mobilization model as a pillar of national defense. The notion of fighting a reprise of World War II was still considered within the realm of the possible.

The gradual abandonment of conscription by the Department of Defense (DoD) coincided with a major shift in the strategic landscape. China and the Soviet Union became embroiled in a rancorous quarrel, while the United States was engaged in Vietnam. Nixon took advantage of this rift and made overtures to both

Peking and Moscow in the early-1970s. The result was a diplomatic revolution. In the new international environment, the threat of nuclear war subsided, while the idea of a monolithic communism bent on expansion lost much of its force.

The Richard Nixon administration revised the national military strategy in light of the new developments. In the place of the old 2 1/2 war strategy, Nixon substituted the 1 1/2 war strategy, focused on Europe and the Persian Gulf. While he cut the size of the Army almost in half in the 4 years after 1969, he planned to use alliances and Allied manpower to compensate for these troop reductions.

The Arab-Israeli War of 1973 greatly affected both U.S. strategy and operational doctrine. The war illustrated the devastating effectiveness of anti-tank and anti-aircraft missiles, which, in combination with other technological innovations, seemed to suggest the superiority of the tactical defense over the offense in conventional operations. Quite possibly, U.S. strategists concluded, the West could blunt a Soviet or North Korean offensive without employing nuclear weapons.

A third watershed in the evolution of the Officer Corps began in the early-1960s and would end with the advent of the All-Volunteer Force (AVF).[29] While the first watershed (the Root Reforms) determined that the professional officer should be broadly trained and versatile and the second (the post-World War II reforms) determined that the Officer Corps would be large, varied, and broadly based, the third suggested that in addition to their other skills, **Army officers should be analytical, lucid, and capable of defending their positions in words and in writing**. If officers did not possess these capabilities and attributes, some

18

feared, they would be overwhelmed and marginalized in a DoD dominated by Secretary of Defense Robert McNamara and his army of systems analysts.[30]

In fact, one of McNamara's first moves as defense chief was to order a review of the Army's system of officer management. The group that conducted that review found a system in disarray; responsibility within the Department of the Army for officer personnel questions was diffused; personnel priorities had not been established; and career managers pursued many separate and short-range objectives. No single agency gave officer management coherence and direction. To remedy these defects, the group called for the elimination of the Office of the Chief of Technical Services and the transfer of officer personnel management to a new organization called the Office of Personnel Operations (OPO). McNamara promptly approved these recommendations. The concentration of all personnel functions in one special staff agency imparted a degree of unity to the management of officers and, some were convinced, to the Army as an institution.

Despite this organizational overhaul, the branch-centered management system remained essentially unchanged. The adjustments changed "who" controlled officer career planning and assignments rather than "how" they would be managed and employed. In short, the basic assumptions that had guided the assignment and career progression of officers since Root's time continued to guide personnel policy.[31]

THE ADVENT OF THE AVF

The volunteer Army that emerged from the tumult of the Vietnam era was smaller, more disciplined, more expensive, more inward-looking, and more tied to the fluctuations of the marketplace than its conscription-based predecessor had been. It came into being at the dawn of what many observers now refer to as the information age. The microchip or integrated circuit, used commercially for the first time in the early-1960s, was, by the late-1970s, beginning to make an impression, albeit a rather weak one, on the economy and business practices.

It took some time for Army leaders as a group to accept and adjust to the idea of an AVF. Many of these leaders regarded the improved living conditions, the relaxed disciplinary standards, and the pay raises that were introduced to attract and retain Soldiers as dysfunctional. Some even saw them as inimical to unit cohesion and the warrior ethos.

General William Dupuy and his followers in the newly formed U.S. Army Training and Doctrine Command (TRADOC) shaped operational doctrine in the 1970s. Dupuy's doctrine of "active defense" envisaged a highly trained professional force blunting a Warsaw Pact offensive in Central Europe through a combination of maneuver and expertly coordinated firepower. "AirLand Battle" replaced the active defense in the early-1980s. This doctrinal construct took the emphasis off the defensive and placed it on the offensive. It also advanced the idea of a "deep battle" as a means of offsetting Warsaw Pact numerical superiority and of disrupting the coherence of its attack. Equipment modernization accompanied these doctrinal initiatives. The "Big Five," consisting of the Abrams tank, the Bradley fighting vehicle, the Apache attack helicopter, the Black Hawk utility helicopter, and the Patriot air defense missile gave the Army what appeared to be a reasonable chance for its doctrine to work.

The Army became much smaller after Vietnam. It went from a force of about 1,500,000 men with 172,000 officers in 1969 to an Army numbering 785,000 men and approximately 90,000 officers in 1975. These reductions were partially offset by increased reliance upon the reserve components. The Total Force Policy, announced by General Creighton Abrams in 1973, embodied this new reliance on the reserves. Under this policy, more than two-thirds of the Army's service support capabilities moved to the AR or NG, making it impractical to engage in extended operations without them. A trimmed back but still robust mobilization infrastructure and a conscription apparatus remained in place to raise vast citizen armies, should the active forces and the reserve components prove insufficient to handle an emergency.

Personnel management in the era of the AVF was very different than it had been in the early-Cold War. After 1973, the Army instituted longer tours, placed greater emphasis on retention, and experienced less turnover than had been the case when it relied on conscripts to fill out its ranks. Moreover, new organizations arose to more efficiently manage recruiting and retention. District Recruiting Commands (later battalions) and ROTC Regions (later brigades) spread cadre across the country in an attempt to keep in contact with the public. Media offensives supplemented these efforts.

With the end of conscription, the Army created a number of commands and agencies to guide its future evolution. TRADOC and the Army Materiel Command (AMC) were two of the more prominent of these organizations. Both TRADOC and AMC cooperated and clashed with their functional counterparts on the Army Staff (the G-3 and G-4, respectively), the jurisdictional boundaries between the two sides being rather vague. An increasing sophistication in testing, analysis, and "consumer" evaluation accompanied the rise of these organizations. Pressure to measure and document output rapidly became an integral part of organizational life.[32]

After the war, and with the example of My Lai and Lieutenant William Calley before it, the Army was wary of relying heavily upon officers without degrees. Consequently, OCS was scaled back, and the ROTC re-emerged as the Army's principal commissioning source. The ROTC came out of the Vietnam war with a reduced profile among the nation's most competitive colleges. Some Army officials worried about the military and social ramifications of this retreat from the nation's centers of intellectual excellence.

The officer management system that emerged after the war had its origins in a study on military professionalism conducted by the USAWC in 1971. The My Lai incident had moved Army Chief of Staff William Westmoreland to launch a complete review of the state of the Officer Corps. Out of this effort came a centralized promotion and command selection process, designated command tours, and primary and secondary specialties for officers. Collectively, these new practices were referred to as the Officer Personnel Management System (OPMS). While it improved the career planning process, OPMS had little effect on the Army's fundamental approach to the employment and development of junior officers.[33]

Approximately 2 years after the introduction of OPMS I (as it was subsequently called), the Army convened yet another board to examine officer education and training needs. The resultant study, A *Review of Education and Training for Officers* (RETO), laid the philosophical foundation for a comprehensive system of career development from pre-commissioning through retirement. The board saw many of its recommendations eventually adopted, although its proposal to institute rigorous intellectual, physical, and psychological screening mechanisms for entry into ROTC proved too difficult and controversial to institute, at least in manner envisioned by the RETO Board.[34]

The Defense Officer Personnel Management Act (DOPMA) of 1980, which replaced the Officer Personnel Act of 1947 as the legislative basis for officer promotions and assignments, was the next major milestone in the history of officer management. Through this legislation, Congress hoped, among other things, to retain officers with scientific and technological talent and afford reasonably uniform career opportunities among the services. Like the OPMS introduced in the 1970s, however, DOPMA represented evolutionary rather than revolutionary change. Built upon legislation from the 1940s and 1950s, some of its key provisions incorporated ideas and policies that had been around since before the turn of the century. DOPMA's restrictiveness bothered many observers. Its provisions relative to assignments, promotions, and retirements were based on time in service and were applied somewhat rigidly across the defense establishment.[35]

In the early-1980s, Army Chief of Staff Edward C. Meyer ordered an assessment of DOPMA's effect on the Officer Corps. The resultant *Professional Development of Officers Study* (PDOS) led to a second iteration of OPMS and more incremental changes to the way the Army managed its officers, i.e., the single branch track, new functional areas, and a revised officer classification system. This study, like those that had preceded it, took aim at pressing contemporary problems.[36] In 1987, General Carl E. Vuono ordered an appraisal of leader development to reconcile the changes in policy and law that had occurred since the introduction of OPMS II with existing officer management practices. This resulted in the *Leader Development Action Plan* (LDAP), which contained over 50 recommendations that were eventually incorporated into OPMS II. With the LDAP, as with similar initiatives in the past, the existing system was refined but not fundamentally altered.[37]

THE POST-COLD WAR ERA

The demise of the Soviet Union and the end of the Cold War created a new international order and greatly altered the strategic situation of the nation. These events occurred at a time when the socioeconomic significance of the transition from the industrial age to the information age was only beginning to be realized. In the Army, only gradually did the full meaning of the information age and the military potential of the microchip dawn on senior leaders.

Shortly after the LDAP was introduced, the Army embarked upon a momentous transformation occasioned by the end of the Cold War. The dissolution of the Soviet Union enabled a dramatic reduction in the size of the Army and its Officer Corps. The Army shrank from about 770,000 troops and 107,000 officers in 1990 to 480,000 troops and 76,000 officers by the end of the century. While these reductions were being effected, certain key pieces of legislation, passed in the late-1980s and early-1990s to address urgent issues that the services were then facing, began to constrain the flexibility of personnel managers. The Goldwater-Nichols Act of 1986 (designed to promote interoperability) and amendments to Titles VIII and XI of the U.S. Code (aimed at closer active and reserve component cooperation) had the effect of narrowing the range of assignment opportunities available to officers.[38]

The post-Cold War draw-down created significant officer management challenges for the Army. A force structure and inventory mismatch, dysfunctional assignment practices, an inflated rating system, a pervasive "zero-defects" mentality, tensions generated by an elevated operational tempo, an erosion of officer warfighting skills, and truncated command tours suggested that something was seriously awry in the way the Army managed and developed its leaders. Critics complained that the Army had a "Cold War" mentality and that its human capital management practices were still rooted in the industrial age. They urged the Army to adapt its outlook and business practices to the requirements of the information age, a term that came into general use in the late-1980s and early-1990s to describe the changes that were transforming the global economy.[39]

To deal with these Officer Corps challenges, then-Chief of Staff Dennis J. Reimer chartered a review of OPMS II. In 1996, he asked Major General David H. Ohle and a team of field grade officers to assess that system's effectiveness in the context of the Army's existing and projected needs. In mid-1997, General Reimer approved a system developed by Ohle's team. Called OPMS III, it was predicated upon developing competency in the Officer Corps. While it left junior officer development virtually untouched, it had a major impact on mid-career officers by grouping interrelated branches and functional areas into four career fields: Operations, Information Operations, Institutional Support, and Operational Support. Under OPMS III, officers competed for promotion only within the same career field, effectively ending the "dual tracking" promotion system which had proved so professionally stultifying in the past.[40]

Some heralded OPMS III as a step in the right direction — it provided alternative career choices and increased the chances for promotion and battalion command for a larger number of officers. Others were less enthusiastic. Some felt that it allowed "operators" to maintain their "stranglehold on flag-level positions," ensuring that specialists and experts remained on the margins of the profession.[41]

In 2000, critics of OPMS III had some of their opinions confirmed when Chief of Staff of the Army General Eric Shinseki entrusted the TRADOC commander with the task of examining how the Army was preparing officers for the challenges of the next century. The Army Training and Leader Development Panel (ATLDP), which performed this task, found that the personnel management system was too focused on meeting "gates" — or in the words of (then) Major General William M. Steele, "placing faces in spaces" — than on quality leader development. The panel also found the Officer Education System (OES) needed revamping. That system, judged as too attuned to Cold

War methods and assumptions, was deemed out of synch with the Army's expanded set of missions and responsibilities.[42]

RECENT DEVELOPMENTS

Since the launch of Operation IRAQI FREEDOM in 2003, the Army has revised its OES in an attempt to align it with the requirements of an extended conflict. Army training and education programs from pre-commissioning to the senior service college level have incorporated lessons learned from Southwest Asia into their curricula. A three-phased Basic Officer Leader Course (BOLC), since revised, was introduced in an attempt to ensure that lieutenants arrived at their first unit of assignment competent in leadership skills, small unit tactics, and branch fundamentals.[43]

As in previous periods of extended conflict, the Army's "mix" of commissioning sources has departed from peacetime patterns. Even before Operation IRAQI FREEDOM, the Army was increasingly relying upon OCS for its junior leaders due to declining officer continuation rates and reduced funding for ROTC. As a result, by 2007, and for the first time since the advent of the AVF, ROTC furnished less than half of the Army's Active-Duty commissioning cohort. Both Congress and senior Army leaders have expressed concern about what this might portend for both the Officer and NCO Corps.

There has been growing recognition in many quarters that the Army needs both a deep and broad distribution of talent in its Officer Corps to meet the demands of the future. At the beginning of this century, the emphasis was on accessing and developing "technologically savvy" officers capable of understanding and managing complex weapons systems. More recently, the call for technologically educated officers has been joined by a demand for culturally sensitive leaders. Consequently, the study of foreign languages and cultures has gained a new salience.

Refinements have continued to be made to the OPMS. Introduced in September 2006, the latest version replaced the four career fields of OPMS III with three new functional categories: Maneuver, Fires and Effects; Operations Support; and Force Sustainment. As in past revisions of the OPMS, however, the changes effected were essentially incremental in nature. The task force that accomplished the revision took what it collectively considered to be a "proven system" and tweaked it so that it could better address current needs.[44]

Over the last decade, calls have been made with increasing frequency to replace the old personnel management system, rooted as it is in the methods and assumptions of the industrial age, with one focused on officer intellectual abilities, bringing the Army on line with the best practices in human capital and enterprise management. It took several centuries for armies to adjust to the new socioeconomic arrangements that replaced the feudal system, and decades for armies to adjust to the demands of the industrial age. How long it will take for armies to adjust to the requirements of the information age is currently a matter of current speculation.[45]

CONCLUSIONS

There is a strong strand of continuity running through the way the Army has managed its Officer Corps over the last century. The Army's officer management policies have undergone frequent revision since 1900, primarily to address issues of contemporary importance. In effecting these revisions, the Army, and in some cases Congress, have taken the existing system as their base and tweaked it to achieve immediately desired outcomes. As a consequence, the current system of officer management has an administrative superstructure consisting of disparate policies and procedures that have accumulated over decades to address specific problems. This patchwork rests upon a foundation built by Root and is firmly rooted in the industrial age. Such an incrementally arrived at officer management system is the antithesis of a coherent strategy. It relies upon a collection of legacy practices when it should instead flow from a conscious and thoughtful planning process designed to meet strategic requirements.

Among other potential causes, the frequent rotation of senior Army officials has disrupted the continuity of leadership needed to formulate and execute such strategic planning. It has also prevented the emergence of a consensus among key leaders about the most fundamental issues affecting the Officer Corps, the absence of which seems particularly debilitating. Key leaders cannot agree: 1) if there is a need for such a strategy; 2) if needed, what elements must be included in that strategy; and 3) if needed, what adjustments are necessary to bring that strategy in line with the information age as the Army looks to the future. In regard to this latter point, some conceive of the information age almost exclusively in technological terms. In their opinion, the Army merely needs to streamline and update a proven system. Others view the information age in the context of a broader social, technological, and economic transformation that demands fundamental changes in the way the Army accesses, develops, retains, and employs talented officers.

Which way the Army eventually decides to go is not at this time clear. Certainly, evolutionary change in its officer management practices has rarely wrought revolutionary results. While the latter has occurred, it has usually taken a military catastrophe or a manifest and dramatic change in external circumstances to induce it. Regardless of which policies emerge from the current debate, one thing is clear — they will shape the Officer Corps for better or worse, throughout much of the ensuing century.

ENDNOTES - CHAPTER 1

1. Casey Wardynski, David S. Lyle, and Michael J. Colarusso, *Accessing Talent: The Foundation of a U.S. Army Officer Corps Strategy*, Carlisle, PA: Strategic Studies Institute, U.S. Army War College, 2010; Casey Wardynski, David S. Lyle, and Michael J. Colarusso, *Towards a U.S. Army Officer Corps Strategy for Success: Developing Talent*, Carlisle, PA: Strategic Studies Institute, U.S. Army War College, 2010; Casey Wardynski, David S. Lyle, and Michael J. Colarusso, *Towards a U.S. Army Officer Corps Strategy for Success: Employing Talent*, Carlisle, PA: Strategic Studies Institute, U.S. Army War College, 2010; Casey Wardynski, David S. Lyle, and Michael J. Colarusso, *Towards a U.S. Army Officer Corps Strategy for Success: Retaining Talent*, Carlisle, PA: Strategic Studies Institute, U.S. Army War College, 2010; Casey Wardynski, David S. Lyle, and Michael J. Colarusso, *Talent: Implications for a U.S. Army Officer Corps Strategy*, Carlisle, PA: Strategic Studies Institute, U.S. Army War College, 2009; and Casey Wardynski, David S. Lyle, and Michael J. Colarusso, *Towards a U.S. Army Officer Corps Strategy for Success: A Proposed Human Capital Model Focused Upon Talent*, Carlisle, PA: Strategic Studies Institute, U.S. Army War College, 2009.

2. Russell F. Weigley, "The Elihu Root Reforms and the Progressive Era," William Geffen, ed., *Command and Commanders*

in Modern Warfare: The Proceedings of the Second Military History Symposium, U.S. Air Force Academy, May 2-3, 1968, Washington, DC: U.S. Government Printing Office (GPO), 1968, pp. 11-27; John Sloan Brown, *Kevlar Legions: Transformation of the U.S. Army, 1989-2005*, Washington, DC: Center of Military History, 2011, p. 10.

3. J. P. Wade *et al.*, *Essay 1: Historical Perspective on the Army Officer Profession*, Washington, DC: Defense Group, Inc., 2008, p. 11.

4. Otto L. Nelson, Jr., *National Security and the General Staff*, Washington, DC: Infantry Journal Press, 1946, pp. 274-276.

5. Brown, p. 8.

6. *Ibid.*, p. 10.

7. *Ibid.*, p. 11.

8. As quoted in James H. Reeves, Jr., *An Army Career Development Plan*, Student Individual Study Project, Carlisle, PA; U.S. Army War College, March 26, 1956, p. 4.

9. Edward M. Coffman and Peter F. Herrly, "The American Regular Army Officer Corps Between the World Wars: A Collective Biography," *Armed Forces and Society*, Vol. 4, November 1, 1977, p. 57.

10. Brown, p. 23.

11. Interview conducted by the author with Mr. William Epley and Dr. Ed Raines, August 19, 2009; Coffman and Herrly, pp. 55-73; John W. Masland and Laurence I. Radway, *Soldiers and Scholars: Military Education and National Policy*, Princeton, NJ: Princeton University Press, 1957, p. 86.

12. Donald P. Snow, *The Golden Age, Vignettes of Military History*, No. 92, Carlisle, PA: U.S. Army Military History Institute, March 6, 1978, p. 3.

13. Memorandum, Office of the Chief of Military History (OCMH), Brigadier General Hal C. Pattison, for Director of Military Personnel, Subject: Quality of the Officer Corps, Washington,

DC: U.S. Army Center of Military History Archives, September 21, 1964.

14. Annual Report of the Chief of Staff, General Douglas MacArthur, For Fiscal Year Ending June 30, 1934, Washington, DC: U.S. Army Center of Military History.

15. Charles E. Kirkpatrick, "Filling the Gaps: Reevaluating Officer Professional Education in the Inter-War Army, 1920-1940," paper presented at the 1989 American Military Institute Annual Conference, April 14-15, 1989, p. 2.

16. George R. Iverson, *Officer Personnel Management: A Historical Perspective*, Strategy Research Project, Carlisle PA: U.S. Army War College, May 1978, p. 10.

17. Coffman and Herrly, pp. 55-73.

18. Brown, p. 22.

19. R. R. Palmer, *The Procurement and Training of Ground Combat Troops*, Washington, DC: U.S. Army Center of Military History, 2003, pp. 87-88; *Department of the Army Pamphlet No. 20-211, The Personnel System in the United States Army*, Washington, DC: GPO, August 1954, p. 234.

20. Palmer, pp. 100-101.

21. Brown, p. 27.

22. *Department of the Army Pamphlet No. 600-3, Career Planning for Army Officers*, Washington, DC: GPO, October 15, 1956, p. 7; Snow, p. 4.

23. Thaddeus Holt, *The Army Officer Corps and the Pentagon in 1965-1967: Miscellaneous Observations*, Thaddeus Holt, Papers, 1 Box, Carlisle, PA: U.S. Army Heritage and Education Center Archives, p. 7.

24. Masland and Radway, p. 20.

25. *Ibid.*, p. 23.

26. Officer Personnel Act of 1947, Hearing on H.R. 3830, 80th Cong., 1st Sess., Senate, Committee on Armed Services, Washington, DC, July 16, 1947, pp. 1-3.

27. Iverson, p. 26.

28. Peter Cappelli, *Talent on Demand: Managing Talent in an Age of Uncertainty*, Boston, MA: Harvard Business Press, 2008, p. 34.

29. The first watershed occurred after the Spanish-American War, while the second occurred after World War II.

30. Holt, p. 14.

31. Iverson, pp. 29, 34.

32. Brown, p. 32.

33. David D. Haught, *Officer Personnel Management in the Army: Past, Present, and Future*, Carlisle PA: U.S. Army War College, April 2003, p. 1.

34. Robert J. Keivit, *U.S. Army Executive Development*, Carlisle, PA: U.S. Army War College, May 1984, p. 1.

35. Peter Schirmer, Harry J. Thie, Margaret C. Harrell, and Michael S. Tseng, *Challenging Time in DOPMA: Flexible and Contemporary Military Officer Management*, Santa Monica, CA: RAND Corporation, 2006, p. xiv.

36. James J. McLeskey III, *The U.S. Army Professional Development Of Officers Study: A Critique*, Carlisle, PA: U.S. Army War College, March 1986, p. 21.

37. Haught, p. 2.

38. *Ibid.*

39. Mary French, "OPMS XXI—An Integrated Strategy," *Army*, Vol. 47, February 1997.

40. *Ibid.*

41. Lloyd Matthews, "The Uniformed Intellectual and his Place in American Arms," *Army*, August 2002, p. 40.

42. William Steele, "Training and Developing Leaders in a Transforming Army," *Military Review*, September-October 2001, p. 3, Haught, p. 17.

43. David C. Hill, *Junior Officer Institutional Leadership Education: Is the Basic Officer Leader Course, (BOLC) Meeting the Challenge?* Carlisle, PA: U.S. Army War College, July 2008, p. 17.

44. Robert P. Stavnes, *Is the Army's Current Force Management System Working?* Carlisle, PA: U.S. Army War College, March 2008, p. 3.

45. Anthony G. Wallace, "Future Directions In Leadership—Implications For The Selection And Development Of Senior Leaders," Master's Thesis, Monterey, CA: Naval Postgraduate School, March 2003, p. 67.

CHAPTER 2

OFFICER TALENT

INTRODUCTION

The Army has never defined officer "talent" in a formal sense. In its official publications and pronouncements over the years, it has instead adduced a laundry list of skills, knowledge, and aptitudes considered critical to mission success. These have changed with shifts in the Army's operating environment and have not been particularly useful as practical guides for officer management. Nevertheless, beginning in the 20th century, there arose within the Army a general concept of talent that, at its core, has remained relatively stable over time and mirrors that found in much of the private sector—that broadly "talented" officers are a small percentage of the force who must be groomed for leadership at the Army's highest levels. In the next several pages, I will attempt to briefly sketch the evolution of the Army's concept of talent (and talent management) since World War I. This chapter was originally intended to accompany the U.S. Military Academy (USMA) Office of Economic and Manpower Analysis (OEMA) monograph entitled *Talent: Implications for a U.S. Army Officer Corps Strategy*, which explores the differences between competent and talented leaders, discusses what talents the U.S. Army should seek in its officers, and lays out a path for the Army to follow to become a truly talent-based organization.[1]

THE INTERWAR PERIOD

The basic blueprint for the system of officer management used by the Army in the interwar period
had taken shape under Secretary of War Elihu Root
in the aftermath of the Spanish-American War. That
system, based upon the Prussian military and corporate production models, entailed rotation between
staff and line assignments and periodic professional
education and training. The assumption was that officers with the desired characteristics and attributes
could be "grown" by putting them through a series
of varied developmental experiences. In the decades
after World War I, those desired characteristics and
attributes were derived from the principal purpose of
the officer management system — to prepare officers
to assume positions of responsibility in the event of
a mass mobilization. Accordingly, the Army's defini-
tion of talent encompassed the attributes of intellectual versatility, adaptability, and what might be called
general leadership and management ability. There
was little room in this scheme for the specialist. The
emphasis was on developing a breadth rather than a
depth of skills, knowledge, and behaviors. Officers
who would occupy key command or staff positions at
the division level and above upon mobilization, after
all, would have to be at least passably conversant with
the wide range of functions necessary for managing
and directing operational units in wartime.[2]

Conditions during the interwar years did not com-
pel the Army to undertake a deeper consideration
of officer talent, at least not in the very overt way it
would after World War II. Due largely to fiscal constraints imposed by a cost-conscious Congress, the

Officer Corps remained relatively small until 1940, its strength hovering between 12,000 and 14,000 officers. Almost all of this rather diminutive force, as it was recognized, would be needed in the event of a national emergency. Consequently, the Army had little occasion to cull poor performers from its ranks. Only egregiously bad officers were cashiered. Neither the promotion system, based primarily on seniority, nor the assignment system, in which personal contacts and general reputation played a huge role, offered clear-cut clues about prevailing military ideas regarding talent.[3]

Some slight insight into the Army's notions about talent, perhaps, can be inferred from a consideration of the so-called plucking boards conducted in 1922 and 1941. The first of these boards was convened to trim the Officer Corps down to a strength level set by Congress. It resulted in the separation of approximately 2,150 officers, from the ranks of lieutenant through colonel. Among the selection criteria used by the board was something called special qualifications, which included, among other things, operational expertise in critical operational or technological fields. Physical fitness and age were other criteria. Officers who no longer possessed the vigor to lead troops in combat or perform arduous peacetime duties were generally the first to be selected for separation from the active ranks. The plucking board held in 1941 also heavily weighted physical vitality. General George Marshall, anticipating the nation's imminent involvement in World War II, wanted to rid the Army of superannuated officers who were not up to the test of combat. He used the plucking board as a winnowing device. In both 1922 and 1941, "talented" officers were viewed as those who would make a spirited, energetic, battle-ready leader.[4] Of note, these boards were not part of a strategic officer management process, but rather reactions to immediate fiscal or national security imperatives.

POST-WORLD WAR II

After the war, the Officer Corps became too large to control in the informal fashion of the interwar years, and more methodical procedures were instituted for the evaluation and promotion of officers. The Officer Personnel Act of 1947 outlawed the practice of blanket promotions based on seniority exclusively and replaced it with a promotion system based on merit (although time in grade restrictions still existed). It also provided for the regularization of the way the Army evaluated officers by introducing a centralized selection board for promotions.[5]

The basic philosophy behind officer management, however, remained the same. To be sure, the Army's ideas about talent took on a more egalitarian aspect, as the interwar ideal of the "officer and gentleman," which had class implications, began to erode. Nevertheless, the Army continued to regard officer qualities and potential as highly malleable and to remain focused on "growing" a particular type of officer. The typical lieutenant entered the Army in his early 20s — at an age when he supposedly had much growth and development ahead of him. The underlying assumption was that through appropriate training, schooling, and mentoring, as well as a variety of developmental assignments, any reasonably intelligent and healthy individual of requisite character could be shaped into a good officer. Indeed, a mythology grew up around historical figures like George Patton, Marshall, and Dwight Eisenhower — officers who did not excel as undergraduates but who went on to careers of extraordinary achievement.[6]

The Army's method for growing officers was very similar to the "company man" system used in corporate America throughout much of the 20th century. This system, which emerged in its fully articulated form in the immediate aftermath of World War II, built managerial talent through a progression of developmental assignments interspersed with training and educational experiences. Mentorship was also often part of the developmental equation. The system was designed to produce versatile and flexible generalists familiar with the entire range of the firm's operations and devoted to a career with that same firm.[7]

Large firms in this era generally eschewed lateral entry, understanding that it created turmoil in the managerial pipeline and placed the firm's corporate culture in peril by inserting the unsocialized into positions of authority. By promoting from within, firms minimized turnover and cultivated an ethos of corporate loyalty and selfless service within their workforce. "Succession planning" for the firm's top executive positions was an important component of that system. In some companies, as Wharton's Peter Cappelli notes, this planning was extremely deep, extending back three generations. It entailed both selection and culling, since fewer and fewer executives were needed as one approached the very top of the career ladder.[8]

The Army's "company man" officer management system functioned reasonably well through the early-1960s. It had critics who complained about its lack of flexibility and precision, but few questioned its essential utility or the philosophical building blocks upon which it rested. The assumption was that the country would rely on a mass citizen Army raised by conscription in the event of a national emergency. It was the job of the personnel system to prepare officers for positions of authority in a defense establishment expanded by mobilization. The emphasis was upon developing broadly knowledgeable and experienced generalists capable of overseeing all aspects of a large military organization.[9]

In practice, the Army's system, like the civilian one it resembled, performed a type of professional triage. The most gifted officers were identified early and groomed for assuming positions of the highest responsibility in wartime. A second group of competent but less talented career officers was prepared for positions of lesser responsibility. A third group, the clearly incompetent, was culled from the service. This system was configured not to align the talent sets of individuals with the requirements of specific positions and to thus raise the level of performance across the Officer Corps, but to identify and develop capable leaders with a breadth of knowledge and experience who could be "plugged into" staff and command billets in wartime.[10]

One contemporary observer has applied the term "cookie cutter" to describe the way the system functioned (and in his opinion, continues to function). The emphasis was on efficiency, simplicity, and the elimination of variables. One personnel manager in the late-1950s likened the Army's personnel management system to a mathematic equation — the fewer variables you have, the easier the equation is to solve. The same individual referred to the officer as a "commodity." When a unit supply officer requisitions jeep tires, he noted, he is not concerned with which tires are placed on which jeeps. He orders and receives a standardized product that can be used on any jeep assigned to the unit. Although he admitted that the personnel manager could not function as a unit supply officer, it was clearly this kind of efficiency that he held up as the ideal. The closer the Army could come to managing officers like interchangeable parts, the more efficient the system would be.[11]

THE TURBULENT 1960s AND EARLY-1970s

The issues confronting personnel managers became progressively more complex in the 1960s and early-1970s. Defense strategy changed, the roles and missions of the Army expanded, and the nation experienced a series of social, economic, and political shocks which reverberated throughout the Armed Forces. In the view of some observers, the Army did not possess the depth of expertise necessary to address adequately the growing array of tasks that it was being called upon to perform. In this environment, the Army was forced to reconsider its ideas about talent and the way it managed its leaders.

It is perhaps more than mere coincidence that the military services began to use the word "talent" in a quasi-systematic way in the early-1960s. Project Talent, a federal program initiated in the late-1950s to inventory and encourage the development of various aptitudes among the young, helped popularize the term in government circles. That project was given a boost by the successful Soviet launch of *Sputnik* in 1958—an event that excited widespread consternation and sparked a host of educational reform initiatives. Psychologist John Flanagan of the American Institute for Research was a force behind Project Talent. Convinced that thousands of Americans were "miscast in

41

the wrong career," he wanted to "pinpoint" the abilities of individual students so that their full potential could be unleashed.[12]

Talent became a part of the U.S. Army War College (USAWC) lexicon in the mid-1960s when, for reasons that will be discussed presently, Army leaders became increasingly sensitive to the need for expert knowledge within the Officer Corps. Some talked of a "talent gap." By this, they meant that the Army did not possess the intellectual capital needed to manage and direct the full range of roles and missions that the nation expected it to. Within segments of the Army school system at least, talent began to be discussed in terms that extended beyond broadly capable leaders to intellectually or technically gifted specialists.[13]

Perhaps the more frequent use of the term among military professionals was related in some way to their growing sense of intellectual inadequacy. Prominent political personages in the 1960s such as John and Robert Kennedy and William Fulbright expressed reservations about the quality of opinion and advice they received from military leaders. In the Pentagon, Secretary of Defense Robert McNamara had changed the terms in which defense questions were framed. During this era, the uniformed services were often at a disadvantage when doing battle with the small army of civilian systems analysts that the secretary had brought to Washington to place defense planning on a more rational basis. Officers often came away from encounters with McNamara's "whiz kids" with a profound sense of their own intellectual inferiority.[14]

The expansion of its responsibilities in the international realm in the late-1960s and early-1970s was one factor behind the Army's new focus on talent. In 1965, Chief of Staff General Harold K. Johnson announced that the Army had a new mission in addition to its traditional ones of defending the nation against external threats and ensuring domestic order. That third mission was nation-building. Confronted with insurgencies and political instability that threatened to alter the international balance of power, political leaders called upon the military services to help friendly governments in the underdeveloped world quell internal disorder and build a foundation for economic and social progress. To fulfill its nation-building mandate, the Army needed officers proficient in foreign languages, conversant with foreign cultures, and capable of performing the many duties and responsibilities encompassed under the rubric of civil affairs.[15]

New domestic missions also affected the Army's view of talent. With the formation of the Department of Defense (DoD) Domestic Action Council (DAC) in April 1969, the services were formally tasked with the mission of assisting other government agencies and private institutions in solving some of the nation's serious domestic problems. Riots, crime, juvenile delinquency, poverty, unemployment, an underperforming educational system, and a host of other societal maladies were, as officials in the Richard Nixon administration pointed out, tearing apart the social fabric of the nation and undermining national security. The Army was called upon to provide officers with the special skills, abilities, and knowledge necessary to assist federal, state, and municipal agencies to administer and develop social programs that could attack these ills.[16]

In 1971, one landmark Army study argued that the sociological and technological revolutions of the late-1960s and early-1970s had major implications for the Officer Corps. The Army faced thorny "sociopsychological" issues that added a new dimension of difficulty and complexity to its search for talent. Of

43

even greater significance for the Officer Corps was the accelerating pace of technological progress, especially progress in the area of computer and information processing technology. The technological advances made during the era were, as various commentators pointed out, fostering the rise of technical economies, altering the external environment in which the services had to operate, and pushing the Army and the rest of society toward increasing specialization. An emerging view was that officers collectively would have to possess a wider and deeper set of skills, aptitudes, and specialized knowledge to deal with these developments.[17]

Army leaders were divided about whether seeking breadth or depth of officer talents was the best way to address the institution's expanded mandate. Some wanted to produce officers who were what a later generation would call "pentathletes" — i.e., officers with both broad and deep talents capable of performing a wide range of duties and functions. Others advocated the development of experts — officers who possessed a depth of knowledge in a particular area. These two competing conceptions of talent co-existed within the ranks of Army leaders without being definitely resolved or reconciled.[18]

There was general agreement among personnel managers that the Army did not have officers with the expertise necessary to address many of its steadily growing list of missions, not in sufficient numbers anyway. Staff officers in the Pentagon reported that they were being bombarded with reports from all levels of command, complaining of a misalignment between the skills that the Army was providing and the skills that were needed in the field. Some urged the Army to revise its personnel management system so that it could place "the right officer possessing the desired qualifications in the right assignment."[19]

Unfortunately for the Army, the company man system was not configured to identify, develop, or retain the type of specific talent that the Army increasingly needed. Standardized career patterns focused on giving the competitive officer a broad exposure to the Army, not on developing special expertise within the Officer Corps. Although there had been a limited drift toward branch functionalism since 1947, officers were still pushed along a career path marked by frequent rotation among a wide variety of assignments and geared toward the production of generalists. In this essentially assignment-based system, there had been little incentive to craft precise descriptions of officer skill requirements or precise definitions of officer qualifications. Thus, positions were not delineated by experience or specific talents, and officer qualifications were normally described only in terms of branch, rank, and occupational specialty, making it extremely difficult for personnel managers to compare skills available with skills needed. In this system, officers with indeterminate skills were assigned to vaguely defined positions.[20]

Even more unfortunately, perhaps, sentiment for change was not powerful or widespread enough to force substantial revisions to what many Army leaders considered to be a proven system. To be sure, there was a growing recognition that, in the words of then Lieutenant Colonel Walter Ulmer, the officer management system had not adapted to "the many changes in the technological, political, and managerial areas of the last 20 years."[21] But tradition, bureaucratic inertia, strategic considerations, and predominate business practices combined to channel the officer management practices along time-worn paths. The Army consequently remained tethered to a "mechanistic" officer management system whose focus was on quickly inserting standardized pegs into standardized holes.

THE ALL-VOLUNTEER FORCE

As the nation emerged from its Vietnam experience and began its experiment with an All-Volunteer Force (AVF), the Army had to contend with momentous changes in the operational environment and in the economic structure of the nation. The traditional concept of preparing officers for positions of responsibility in the event of mobilization, while still very potent, began to erode. It was increasingly challenged by a strategic precept that called for the nation's defense forces to be maintained in a high state of readiness. The lethality of the modern battlefield as evidenced in the 1973 Arab-Israeli War suggested that the nation needed a force capable of massing its full power at the onset of a crisis.[22]

An even more significant development occurred in the economic arena. The company man system, which had informed business practices in the industrial age, began to fall apart in the 1970s as new technology, competition from abroad, and better cost accounting methods reduced the ability of and incentives for firms to forecast market conditions and develop talent matched to the new environment. A rash of mergers and corporate takeovers interacted with a series of macroeconomic shocks in the form of rapidly rising energy prices, inflation, and interest rates to disrupt whole businesses along with established business practices. To stay afloat, large firms began to accelerate their rate of adaptation, ending existing lines of business and starting new ones.[23]

This more dynamic environment caused corporate development and retention of talent to give way to talent poaching from competitors as the demand for information and knowledge producing employees exploded. In turn, firms also had to jettison employees whose talents were no longer in demand. The rapid pace of change compelled organizations to make quick adjustments to their staffs, either to cut costs or add capacity. Change was accelerated by the increasing proclivity of employees at the bottom of the career ladder, who could now look elsewhere for promotion and advancement.[24]

As civilian firms changed their business practices and talent management systems over the course of the next 2 decades, the Army basically held fast to its tried and true methods. To be sure, incremental changes were regularly made to the system. General William Westmoreland implemented the first Officer Personnel Management System (OPMS) in the early-1970s in response to the My Lai incident, the social and political ferment of the 1960s, and the increasing need for specialized knowledge. The first version of OPMS introduced centralized command selection and a system of primary and secondary specialties for officers. The Defense Officer Personnel Management Act (DOPMA) of 1980 was crafted to, *inter alia*, retain scientific and technical talent in the Officer Corps. In the early-1980s, OPMS II introduced single tracking, multiple career paths, and a revised officer classification system. At the end of the decade, the Leader Development Action Plan brought OPMS II on line with the latest changes in law, policy, and procedures. Still, despite these attempts to create more flexible career patterns for officers, the divide between the best talent management practices of the business community and those of the Army widened. While many civilian firms drastically revised their systems of talent management in response to increasingly intense global competition, the Army continued to force its officers along fairly narrow and inflexible career paths that emphasized branch qualification and featured a series of short-term assignments. It continued, in other words, to embrace a system oriented toward achieving efficiency in administration and addressing immediate operational requirements.[25]

AFTER THE COLD WAR

The end of the Cold War brought with it another reordering of the strategic and economic landscape. With the demise of the Soviet Union and the emergence of a unipolar world, the specter of a war requiring a mass mobilization receded further into the background. At the same time, the range of missions and responsibilities, along with the number of deployments, began to proliferate. The initiation of a global counterterrorism campaign in the early-21st century again expanded the scope of the Army's responsibilities, as well as the breadth and depth of officer talents necessary to meet them.[26]

At the same time, the "mechanistic, bureaucratic" business model of the industrial age was clearly on the way to extinction. Hierarchy was fading away and the precise delineations that had marked out the internal structure of corporations were becoming harder to discern. Traditional titles and departmental designations often disappeared or took on new meanings. Flexible, knowledge-based organizations came to dominate the business world.[27]

As it had in the past, the Army revised its personnel system to accommodate contemporary demands. To meet the challenges of the post-Cold War drawdown, it introduced OPMS III in 1997. The new system, expressly designed to ensure competency in the Officer Corps, grouped interrelated branches and functional areas into four career fields, effectively ending the "dual tracking" model of career development that many officers found so debilitating. In 2006, the Army again refined the system by replacing the four career fields elaborated under OPMS III with three new functional categories.[28]

Through it all, the Army's basic approach to, and philosophy about, officer career development and talent management remained basically the same. In 2005, the Army's prevailing notions about talent were encapsulated in the concept of the "pentathlete." Under this concept, talent was associated with innovative, adaptive, culturally astute leaders who were well-versed in a range of disciplines. Pentathletes were to master their core career competencies and, along the way, develop expertise in the broader, more complex politico-military arena. This vision of officer talent was in many respects similar to the one articulated by the creators of the OPMS in the early-1970s. Both visions took the development of the versatile generalist as their baseline and superimposed requirements for specialized knowledge on top of that foundation. The emphasis in both visions was clearly on shunting officers through standardized gates rather than liberating the available talent in the Officer Corps. Accordingly, career patterns changed relatively little. The professional lives of most officers continued to lead down the familiar paths, and the principal object of personnel managers continued to revolve around "placing faces in spaces." It was an approach and a philosophy firmly rooted in the industrial age and industrial age business practices and in Cold War strategic concepts.[29]

Because the American domestic labor market had evolved beyond industrial era practices, however, the Army found itself in an increasingly difficult competition for American talent, and its officers now had a greater range of external employment options available to them than ever before.

CONCLUSION

The Army's general concept of talent has remained relatively stable over the last century—that broadly talented officers are a small percentage of the force that must be groomed for leadership at the Army's highest levels. That thinking has been bound up closely with an officer management system that emphasizes short-term operational assignments encompassing a broad range of duties and experiences. Versatility, flexibility, and general leadership ability have been the traits and attributes that have made for professional success. Little importance has been attached to the idea of liberating the breadth **and** depth of talent available within the Officer Corps.

The system has come under increasing stress as economic and strategic conditions have changed over the last 40 years. The decreasing likelihood of a mass mobilization, the expanding range of the Army's missions and responsibilities since the end of the Vietnam war, and, most significantly, the fundamental changes in business practices that have occurred as the national economy has evolved from the industrial age to the information age accounts for most of this stress.

To date, the Army's attempts to accommodate these trends have not altered the essential character of the system. The way the Army manages and views its officers remains tied to an economic model that, in the civilian world, is becoming increasingly outmoded. It is a model that has not, for the most part, permitted the Army with any degree of consistency and regularity to place the right officer with the right skills in the right position. Creating an officer talent management system that can compete in a conceptual-age labor market and also meet the full range of missions and responsibilities facing the Army is clearly one of the more urgent tasks facing its leadership today.

ENDNOTES - CHAPTER 2

1. Author interview with Mr. William Epley, Washington, DC, U.S. Army Center of Military History, October 30, 2009; Casey Wardynski *et al.*, *Talent: Implications for a U.S. Army Officer Corps Strategy*, Carlisle, PA: Strategic Studies Institute, U.S. Army War College, November 2009.

2. Edward M. Coffman, *The Regulars: The American Army, 1898-1941*, Cambridge, MA: Belknap Press of Harvard University Press, 2004, p. 191.

3. Forrest C. Pogue, *George C. Marshall: Ordeal and Hope*, New York: The Viking Press, 1966, p. 95; Martin Blumenson, "America's World War II Leaders in Europe: Some Thoughts," *Parameters*, December 1989, pp. 2-13; Brigadier General Andrew Muses, *The Personnel Division of the War Department General Staff*, Lecture Delivered at the U.S. Army War College, Carlisle, PA, October 9, 1934; Brigadier General Hal C. Patterson, Chief of Military History For Director of Personnel, OCMH, ODCSPER, Memorandum, Subject: Quality of the Officer Corps, September 21, 1964.

4. "Army Officers Mourn Over 'Plucking' of 2,500: Dickman Board Begins Today Unwelcome Task of Selection from Efficient Force," *New York Times*, July 25, 1992; Pogue, pp. 91-101; "Senate

Group Reports Army's 'Plucking' Bill," *Army and Navy Journal,* July 12, 1941, pp. 1283-1284; "Army's 'Plucking' Bill Approved by Congress," *Army and Navy Journal,* July 26, 1941, p. 1337.

5. George R. Iverson, *Officer Personnel Management: A Historical Perspective,* Strategy Research Project, Carlisle, PA: U.S. Army War College, May 1978, pp. 14-21.

6. Jane M. Arabian and Jennifer A. Shelby, "Policies, Procedures, and People: The Initial Selection of U.S. Military Officers," *Officer Selection,* Nueilly-Sur-Seine Cedex, France: NATO Research and Technology Organization, 2000, pp. I-7.

7. Peter Cappelli, *Talent on Demand: Managing Talent in an Age of Uncertainty,* Boston, MA: Harvard Business Press, 2008, pp. 9-10.

8. *Ibid.,* pp. 19-20.

9. James Burk, "Military Mobilization in Modern Western Societies," Guiseppe Carforio, ed., *Handbook of the Sociology of the Military,* New York: Kluwer Academic/Plenum Publishers, 2003, p. 111.

10. Edward Bautz, Jr., *Imponderables of Officer Personnel Management,* Strategy Research Project, Carlisle, PA: U.S. Army War College, March 1958, p. 15.

11. Kevin Stringer, *The War on Terror and the War for Officer Talent: Linked Challenges for the U.S. Army,* Arlington, VA: Association of the United States Army, July 2008, p. 1; Bautz, p. 41.

12. "Education: Talent Census," *Time Magazine,* August 24, 1962, available from *www.time.com/time/magazine/article/0,9171,896531-1,00.html*; J. Flanagan, J. Daily, M. Shaycroft, M. Gorham, W. Orr, and D. Goldberg, "Identification, Development, and Utilization of Talent," Washington, DC: American Institute for Research, June 1, 1960; and "Project Talent," Pittsburgh PA: University of Pittsburgh, May 12, 1961; M. Shaycroft, C. Neyman, and J. Daily, "Comparison of Navy Recruits with Male High School Students on the Basis of Project Talent Data," Washington, DC: American Institute for Research, June 1, 1962.

13. Robert J. Baer, *Are We Trimming the Fat or Wasting Needed Talent?* Student Essay, Carlisle, PA: U.S. Army War College, April 1967, p. 11.

14. Samuel P. Huntington, "Power, Expertise, and the Military Profession," *Daedalus*, Fall 1963, p. 785.

15. Harold K. Johnson, "The Army's Role in Nation Building and Preserving Stability," *Army Information Digest*, November 1965, pp. 6-13.

16. Robert E. Ayers, *Army Talent in the Domestic Arena*, Student Research Report, U.S. Army War College, March 1970, p. 2; U.S. Secretary of Defense Melvin R. Laird, Memorandum for Secretaries of the Military Departments, Subject: Domestic Action Council, Washington, DC, April 28, 1969.

17. Frank W. Norris, *Review of Army Officer Educational System*, Vol. II, Full Report and Annexes B, C, December 1, 1971, pp. 2-1 to 2-10.

18. Baer, p. 12; John J. Briscoe, *Is the Army Forfeiting Officer Talent?* Student Essay, Carlisle, PA: U.S. Army War College, April 1967, p. 5.

19. Briscoe, p. 5.

20. Walter F. Ulmer, Jr., *Concepts of Generalization and Specialization in Officer Career Management*, Student Thesis, Carlisle, PA: U.S. Army War College, March 1969, pp. 34, 43.

21. *Ibid.*, p. 50.

22. Burk, p. 117.

23. Cappelli, p. 28.

24. *Ibid.*

25. David D. Haught, *Officer Personnel Management in the Army: Past, Present, and Future*, Strategy Research Project, Carlisle, PA: U.S. Army War College, April 2003, p. 1.

26. Burk, p. 118.

27. Wayne E. Whiteman, *Training and Educating Army Officers for the 21st Century: Implications for the United States Military Academy*, Student Research Paper, Carlisle, PA: U.S. Army War College, March 1998, p. 11.

28. Mary French, "OPMS XXI—An Integrated Strategy," *Army*, Vol. 47, February 1997; Robert P. Stavnes, *Is the Army's Current Force Management System Working?* Carlisle, PA: U.S. Army War College, March 2008, p. 3.

29. Robert A. Tipton, *Professional Military Education for the "Pentathlete" of the Future*, Strategy Research Project, Carlisle, PA: U.S. Army War College, March 2006, pp. 8-9; William Steele, "Training and Developing Leaders in a Transforming Army," *Military Review*, September-October, 2001, p. 3.

CHAPTER 3

RETAINING OFFICER TALENT

INTRODUCTION

Officer attrition is a problem that intermittently has afflicted the Officer Corps since the conclusion of World War II. Over this period, the Army frequently has struggled to retain not only the requisite number of officers, but "talented" officers as well. The retention of junior officers has posed a particularly difficult challenge and, from time to time over the last 6 decades, has attracted a great deal of both public and official scrutiny. Accordingly, the focus of this chapter will be on the attrition problem among captains and lieutenants.

Because the Army's officer retention problems after 1980 have been covered in considerable detail in a Strategic Studies Institute monograph by Casey Wardynski, David Lyle, and Mike Colorusso, the scope of discussion here is limited to developments before 1980, when "industrial age" management practices were very much in the ascendancy in both the military services and civilian firms. First is a look at the Officer Corps and officer retention patterns in the interwar period—the period in which many of the senior officers who would lead the Army in the 1950s, 1960s, and even into the 1970s were introduced to the military profession. A basic familiarity with conditions in the interwar Army is a prerequisite for fully appreciating the effects of the changes that took place after 1945.

THE INTERWAR PERIOD

Persuading officers to remain in the Army in the 2 decades after the conclusion of World War I was generally not a problem. In fact, throughout the interwar years, and especially after the onset of the Great Depression in 1929, the officer retention environment was very auspicious. Accessions standards were high. To obtain a commission, officer aspirants, except for those who graduated from the U.S. Military Academy (USMA), had to pass rigorous examinations designed to measure academic and intellectual attainment. The Army had many more applicants for commissions than it had vacancies in the Officer Corps. Competition for lieutenancies was consequently intense, commissions were highly valued, and resignations were relatively infrequent.[1]

The Army offered what most Americans during the Depression years undoubtedly considered to be a very attractive compensation package to its officers. Officers received adequate and sometimes highly desirable housing, free medical and dental care both for themselves and their families, an assured and sufficient salary, a retirement income after 30 years of satisfactory service, and free life insurance. In addition, perquisites such as commissary and post exchange privileges provided real value to officers' families. Post exchanges, which were exempt from national and local taxes, offered substantial savings on a variety of items. Commissaries, too, helped the officer stretch his salary by providing significant discounts on groceries and other household goods.[2]

Professionally, the interwar Army provided a satisfying experience. Junior officers were placed in responsible and challenging jobs and allowed considerable initiative in the performance of their duties. Indeed, they were encouraged to work independently. Any mistakes and shortcomings in the performance of their duties were usually dealt with informally with a personal counseling session by their commander. Pressures to maintain a high state of readiness and what later generations would refer to as a "zero-defects" mentality were largely unknown. The Officer Corps, like the typical Army post, was small and close knit. A cohesive military society produced through enforced isolation and rigorous selection helped to engender an Officer Corps distinguished by its expertise, group identification, homogeneity, and sense of corporateness. For many in this self-contained world, a military career had overtones of a calling.[3]

The quality of life in the interwar Army was generally quite good. The officer led what one historian characterized as a "country club existence." His social standing was quite high—comparable to that of an upper middle class professional in the civilian community. Although officers and their wives were expected to take part in an almost continuous round of social engagements, the burden of preparing for these events (along with the burden of performing many of the heavier household chores) was lightened by enlisted orderlies, who were able to add substantially to their income by moonlighting as domestic help. Family separations, when they did occur, were usually brief. Officers would, for the most part, be away from their homes only during training exercises. Families almost always accompanied officers on tours of duty in foreign stations. Moreover, the officer generally maintained a 30-hour work week, delegating much of the unit's routine administration to noncommissioned officers (NCOs). He consequently had plenty of time to spend with his wife and children, as well as plenty of time to read, reflect, and get involved in sports and other activities.[4]

THE POST-WORLD WAR II ERA

As the dynamics of military service changed after World War II, the attractiveness of a military career declined sharply. This led to an exodus of junior officers from the ranks. By the early-1950s, officer attrition had become so worrisome that some were calling it a "threat to national security." Top civilian and military leaders talked frankly and openly about the problem, and the press devoted considerable attention to it. President Harry Truman appointed the Strauss Committee to look into the matter in 1949, while his Secretary of Defense convened a Citizens' Advisory Commission headed by Harold Moulton of the Brookings Institution for the same purpose the following year. In the first year of the Dwight Eisenhower administration, the Rockefeller Committee (1953) and the Womble Committee (1953) addressed the problem of officer attrition. Both of these bodies issued grave warnings about what might ensue if the Army did not take prompt action to retain its young career personnel. President Eisenhower himself weighed in on the issue in 1955 when he sent a message to the House of Representatives deploring the loss of junior officers and enlisted personnel and suggesting ways to stop the hemorrhaging.[5]

The massive influx of officers into the force during World War II had added to the Army's junior officer troubles by creating a 5-year "hump" of excessive officer strength during 1941 through 1945. This hump interacted with frequent reductions in officer strength (especially after the introduction of Eisenhower's New Look strategy in the early-1950s) and the Army's proclivity to effect officer reductions by cutting accessions to produce a pronounced misdistribution of ranks. By the early-1950s, the Army had many older and far fewer younger officers than it needed.[6]

The greatest number of officer resignations occurred among lieutenants and captains within 2 years after they had completed their initial service obligation. Shortly after the Korean war ended, the Army permitted certain Regular Army (RA) officers to resign. Among junior RA captains, the resignation rate was "alarming." In less than 1 year, 30 percent of this group submitted resignations. The resignation rate of other than RA (OTRA) lieutenants was even more disquieting. Throughout the 1950s, in fact, only 15 percent of the reserve lieutenants produced through Reserve Officer Training Corps (ROTC) and Officer Candidate School (OCS) volunteered to remain in the Army after their 2 years of compulsory service. Steps were taken, from time to time, to induce these men to accept RA commissions. These efforts were ineffectual, however. Resolved to get out of the service at the first opportunity, lieutenants strenuously avoided incurring a longer term of service.[7]

The dearth of quality in the Officer Corps was considered an even bigger problem than the lack of quantity. In 1954, the Senate Armed Services Committee stated:

> The Army is today faced with a most critical and delicate problem. It is becoming increasingly more difficult to attract and hold within the career services high-caliber men and women.[8]

One Army War College student wrote in 1956 that the Officer Corps was of the "lowest . . . quality in Army history." The 15 percent of ROTC graduates who elected to remain in the Army, he noted, were from the lower ranges of their cohorts in terms of intellect and ability.[9]

The growth in the Officer Corps in World War II had forced the Army to lower its intellectual and educational standards for commissioning. The emphasis by necessity was on quantity, not quality. As commissioning standards fell, so, too, did moral and behavioral standards. Breaches of accepted professional conduct became commonplace. To meet the needs of the force in the post-war era, the RA, which had procured virtually 100 percent college graduates from 1920 through 1940, integrated 4,574 of the non-degreed officers who had been commissioned during the war into its ranks in 1947 and 1948. Input from the newly reactivated ROTC program did little to raise officer quality. The rapid fall in service attractiveness had led to the entry of many "lower caliber individuals" into the Army through ROTC, despite the fact that all of them were college graduates. The Army's power of attraction was so low that it could exercise little or no discretion over who it let in or who it retained in the officer ranks.[10]

Some argued that the Army's officer retention troubles were due in part to the many "low caliber" officers that it had to retain. Capable junior officers could not help but notice that many of their superior officers were considerably less educated and intelligent than were they. Moreover, rank, along with the officer's commission, had supposedly been "cheapened" by the Army's conferring both on "countless incompetent people." To attract and retain high caliber officers, some argued, the Army had to do a better job of vetting officer candidates and culling the incompetent from the Officer Corps.[11]

Pay and standard of living issues were widely held to be among the most important factors dissuading the talented from remaining in the Army. The Cordiner Report noted that a career in business or commerce generally offered greater financial rewards and more occupational freedom than service as an officer. The Army was simply unable to give the talented young officer the pay, stability, prestige, promotion opportunities, and the perquisites of a civilian firm.[12]

Officers were very aware that military pay and benefits had steadily eroded since the interwar years. The major of 1930, one Army War College student asserted, had a higher standard of living than the colonel of 1953. After the war, the officer had rapidly lost ground to his contemporaries in government, commerce, and business. Military pay raises in the late-1940s and early-1950s lagged far behind those accorded other segments of the workforce. Even the modest pay increases that officers did receive were offset to a degree by the elimination of certain longstanding perquisites such as the military tax exemption on $1,500 of base pay and the 10 percent supplement for overseas duty.[13]

Traditional compensatory benefits and services, such as those which the post exchange and commissary at one time provided, also markedly deteriorated after the war. As a result of a study by the House Armed Services Committee (HASC) in 1949, the military services placed restrictions on the kind of merchandise which could be sold, added a 5 percent charge on purchases at commissaries to cover overhead costs, and abolished the exemption from excise taxes on many items. Civilian shopping centers could now match, and in some cases even beat, post exchange and commissary prices.[14]

Other benefits that made for a good quality of life were abolished or scaled back after the war. Family housing emerged as a pressing concern for officers and their families, as the Cold War growth of the Army resulted in serious shortages of on-post quarters. Most officers became commuters, living in the civilian community where they were often unable to find or afford accommodations comparable to those that existed on post. With this move off post, the Army community lost much of its cohesiveness and sense of unity. Medical treatment became problematic as well, due to, among other things, a shortage of physicians. Access to medical care was often available only on a limited basis depending on the situation at each duty station. Dental care for dependents was virtually eliminated after 1956. Life insurance, which until 1951 had been provided free to officers, now had to be purchased. Family separation, virtually unknown during the interwar years, became a near universal experience as the stationing of units overseas accelerated in the 1950s. Officers now had to contend with unaccompanied short tours at foreign stations at irregular intervals throughout their career. Annual leave and leisure time were other casualties. A heightened operational tempo and a new sense of urgency resulted in many officers forfeiting their accumulated leave, with both their family time and psychological well-being often suffering as a result. Finally, officers lost many of the little benefits that they possessed during the interwar period, such as orderlies and certain club privileges. The upshot of this was that officer families could no longer experience the genteel lifestyle of their predecessors.[15]

A loss of prestige associated with being an officer also reputedly worked against retention. Public pressure and inductee discontent had brought about a democratization of the Army during the war. Practices accepted as routine in the interwar Army were not appropriate in the mass citizen Army created for the fight against Germany and Japan. Service leaders were forced to adopt policies that diminished the distinctions between ranks and the social gulf between the officer and the enlisted man.

In the immediate aftermath of the war, the turmoil caused by demobilization, the unsettled state of the world, and the complaints of disgruntled civilian Soldiers who had the misfortune to serve under incompetent or overbearing officers created a morale problem. The Army's action at this time was to appoint the Doolittle Board to study officer-enlisted man relationships and make recommendations to the Secretary of War. The upshot of this effort was that many of the regulations, customs, and traditions that had perpetuated the social and profession divide between the commissioned and enlisted ranks were eliminated.[16]

The conditions of service, too, worked against the retention of capable officers. During the interwar period, officers were given challenging tasks and allowed to work semi-autonomously with but a minimum of supervision by senior officers. The expansion of the Army in the post-war era, together with the escalation of international tensions brought on by the Cold War, had changed the dynamics of service. The Officer Corps was transformed from a small, integrated, and relatively homogeneous body into a large, diverse, and transient collection of individuals. The new urgency and constant state of tension that the Cold

War brought to military life drove the Army toward the centralization of command and control. Training became rigidly controlled by detailed directives and schedules from higher headquarters. Junior officers were held on a very short leash and not allowed to exercise their judgment or initiative in their work. Because units now had to maintain a high state of readiness, not even routine matters could be left to chance. Junior officers were now required to attend to many housekeeping chores that had been left to corporals and sergeants in the interwar years. The deleterious effects of centralization and over-supervision were compounded by overwork — another outgrowth of the perpetual state of urgency occasioned by the operational demands of the Cold War. Young officers found themselves working 50-, 60-, or even 70-hour weeks, sacrificing their family life for the sake of their menial and oftentimes unnecessary duties.[17]

The officer personnel management system added to the frustration of the most able captains and lieutenants. The large part that seniority played in promotion killed initiative in the truly ambitious and dissuaded them from remaining in the service. Moreover, the emphasis in this system was not on managing junior officer careers but on "filling spaces with faces." Lieutenants were regarded as interchangeable parts and treated like requisitioned items in the supply system. Little thought was given to their professional development or to their goals and abilities.[18]

To boost retention rates, the Army adopted a number of measures designed to improve the lot of junior officers. Periodic pay raises, enhanced survivor benefits, the stabilization of assignments, the abbreviation of hardship tours, increased career counseling, and accelerated promotions for the most competitive officers were some of the initiatives adopted.[19]

While welcomed, the adopted measures did not have the desired effect on retention rates. The measures taken, after all, were quite limited in scope, dealing primarily with organization, career counseling, and pay. While the periodic pay increases attained during the 1950s were eagerly accepted by junior officers, they were not of a nature or of a magnitude that could lure top quality officers away from civilian firms, which could still offer far more generous compensation packages than the Army. To make matters worse, advantage was not taken of those opportunities that did present themselves. The 1958 pay raise legislation had given the Army the ability to affect the retention equation in a significant fashion. Passed in the wake of the Soviet launch of *Sputnik,* it authorized the services to grant targeted increases to certain specialists who were in critically short supply. While the Navy and Air Force took advantage of this legislation, the more egalitarian Army did not. Absorbed in the cult of the generalist and the company man approach to officer personnel management, it chose to grant across the board pay hikes and spread the financial rewards evenly among all segments of the Officer Corps.[20]

Efforts to raise retention rates also suffered from a lack of holistic and systematic analysis of the various factors (along with the relationship among those factors) that influenced the career decisions of junior officers. The studies that were conducted by the various boards and organizations that looked into the retention issue were, for the most part, ad hoc affairs that lacked depth, breadth, and scientific rigor. Moreover, none of these efforts attempted to articulate a holistic strategy that took into account the full range of factors that impacted retention.[21]

VIETNAM

Officer retention resurfaced as a major issue during the Vietnam war. To be sure, it had never really disappeared. The exodus of junior officer talent that began in the late-1940s continued largely unabated into the early-1960s (although that flow was subject to, *inter alia*, intermittent fluctuations of the unemployment rate). Concern among senior Army leaders waxed in the late-1960s and early-1970s as the exodus of junior officers from Active Duty reached what many observers considered to be crisis proportions. The high turnover rate not only represented a loss of valuable military experience and a reduction in the overall ability and proficiency of the Army, it greatly increased costs and contributed to a rising defense budget, which had become a matter of great concern to lawmakers by the late-1960s.

The officer retention rate fell dramatically over the course of the 1960s. OCS retention rates sank from 71.7 percent in 1960 (a year when OCS input into the Army was very limited) to 33.8 percent in 1969 (by which time OCS had become the Army's single largest accessions source). The slumping rate of extensions by OCS commissioned officers was explained in part by the increasing numbers of college graduates who entered OCS to avoid enlisted service but who had no intention of making the Army a career.[22]

The retention rate for ROTC officers was even worse. That rate for OTRA ROTC officers decreased from 24.2 percent in 1960 to just 11.2 percent in 1970. Even more worrisome to the Army, the retention rates of Distinguished Military Graduates (DMGs) were equally as low. Many ROTC graduates, like OCS graduates, were draft-induced volunteers with little inclination to make the Army their career. The situation with ROTC officers was considered so serious that real consideration was given to replacing ROTC with a more cost-effective commissioning program.[23]

Although retention rates among USMA graduates were somewhat better, the rate at which they were leaving the Army was still distressing. USMA rates were bolstered throughout much of the 1960s by two factors. First, the USMA admitted more prior service cadets in the 1960s—and in this era, they had a higher propensity to remain in the service. Second, in Fiscal Year (FY) 1966, the Army instituted a Selective Retention Program that had an involuntary component. The program was designed to retain on a selective basis those individuals needed to support the buildup of the active Army who otherwise would have been lost through voluntary retirement, resignation, or relief from Active Duty. When the Involuntary Retention Program was terminated in December 1969, the resignation rates of the West Point classes 1963 through 1965 shot up and exceeded historical norms.[24]

Once again in the Vietnam era, however, the lack of quality among junior officers was considered to be an even bigger problem than the lack of quality. The Army, one U.S. Army War College (USAWC) student bluntly asserted, does not "retain outstanding officers in large numbers." Top quality lieutenants and captains were leaving the service in "alarming numbers" and officers in the Officer of the Deputy Chief of Staff for Personnel (ODCSPER) were not optimistic about reversing the trend. Even the Army ROTC scholarship program, instituted in 1964 to raise the qualitative input of the ROTC program, it was concluded, was not attracting the "talented and educated young men" that the Army hoped to procure and retain as career officers.[25]

In an effort to stem the flow of junior officers out of the service, the Army conducted and sponsored a number of studies designed to determine what type of individual stayed in the service and what type left. The Army found, not surprisingly, that education and socioeconomic background were related inversely with propensity to pursue a career as an officer. The higher the education level of the captain or lieutenant, the more likely he was to seek civilian employment. Junior officers with less than 2 years of college were more than twice as likely to make the Army a career as those with a baccalaureate degree, and three times as likely as those with a master's degree or above. The more intelligent and educated officer, the Army concluded, was less likely to pursue a career because he was more aware of alternatives.

At the same time, officers from affluent neighborhoods, it was found, were less likely to stay in the Army than those from poor or lower middle class communities. The material aspirations of the less affluent could be met through a military career while those of the upper middle class could not. Geography and marital status also figured into the retention matrix. Junior officers who grew up in rural areas were more likely to remain in the Army than those from urban communities and married officers, especially those with children, had much higher retention rates than single officers.[26]

Some linked the Army's retention difficulties to the social and political turmoil of the era. In an age of urban riots, student demonstrations, and widespread social unrest, it seemed that anti-military attitudes and demands for greater individual freedom permeated the educated segments of society. Such an environment did nothing to encourage military service.

Still, some pointed out, the turmoil surrounding the Vietnam war had less influence on junior officer retention than many supposed. There were other factors that were far more important in shaping the career intentions of junior officers than this turmoil.[27]

Many of the factors that had negatively affected retention in the 1950s and early-1960s were still present, although some had taken on at least a slightly different aspect. One such factor was pay. The more highly educated or technically trained junior officers often felt that they were given duties that were beneath their level and that they should receive more pay than less skilled or educated officers. They also perceived the Army pay system to be inflexible and excessively bureaucratic. That system did not compensate for performance variables such as level of responsibility, long hours, and the quality of work performed. Promotion continued to be an issue. Civilian firms generally placed more emphasis on performance and less on seniority than the Army.[28]

Family separations, frequent moves, and lack of leisure time likewise remained as important impediments to retention. One Army survey conducted during this period found that the most unpopular and negative aspects of Army life from the perspective of the junior officer's wife were family separations and frequent moves. For the officer who decided to leave the service, the lack of leisure time ranked high on his list of reasons for leaving.[29]

The low prestige of the military profession became even more salient as a retention factor during the period under review. While much of this was attributable to trends over which military leaders had no control, the Army itself contributed to the diminution of prestige. The rapid promotions that occurred during the

Vietnam war (some officers made major with only 5 years of service) and the erosion of accessions standards certainly hurt the image of the Officer Corps. Increasingly, the large number of marginally qualified officers that the Army accessed and promoted to lead an expanded force drove many of the most capable officers out of the service.[30]

The lack of opportunity for Reserve officers, who made up the bulk of the Officer Corps, contributed to the retention problem as well. To be sure, Army leaders expressed dismay that only a small fraction (about 16 percent in the late-1960s) of Reserve officers, or OTRA officers as they were designated, remained on Active Duty after their initial service obligation expired. At the same time, however, the Army gave the OTRA junior officer a distinctly second class status. Upon his entry into the active Army, the OTRA officer recognized that for him, the career opportunities and tenure of service were far more dubious than for RA officers. As OTRA officers, they soon became aware that their retention on Active Duty depended highly on the periodic reductions in force effected to stay within fluctuating officer ceilings. For the most part, chances for advanced civilian education, attendance at a senior service college, and landing a career-enhancing job were remote. These inequities, coupled with the fact that many OTRA officers sought a commission in order to avoid service as an enlisted man, resulted in the low retention rates of this group.[31]

According to the Deputy Chief of Staff for Personnel (DCSPER) the biggest single obstacle to officer retention continued to be a lack of job satisfaction. As it was, most junior officers had little scope for independent action and hence little opportunity to develop a sense of self-worth or self-importance. Nor did the jobs to which they were assigned generally afford them responsibility, provide them with a sense of accomplishment, or present them with a challenge.[32]

As we have seen, one of the reasons for this state of affairs was the elevated state of combat readiness required by the Cold War. Commanders had to train according to centralized training directives, prepare their organizations to deploy on short notice, and certify on a quarterly basis the quantifiable readiness condition of their unit. Pressed to achieve near perfection even in routine matters, they expected junior officers to oversee personally many menial tasks for which they were held accountable. Junior officers saw themselves as tethered to the supervision of tedious and often trivial duties and work details, subjected to hectic and harassing working conditions, and deprived of opportunities for individual initiative and development.[33]

Even more troubling to junior officers was the fact that their jobs and Military Occupational Specialties (MOS) were generally inconsistent with their skills, career interests, educational qualifications, or military training. For those officers with highly specialized educations, the inability of the Army to use their qualifications and skills served as a huge disincentive for retention. Although some branches tried to assign officers to jobs that matched their skills or educational background, the odds of actually making such a match were quite small.[34]

Factors that inhibited the Army from aligning jobs with skills, education, and military training included: 1) the Army's preference for the generalist; in the company man system that guided officer management, there was little room for the highly educated, technically trained junior officer who wanted to use his special skills; 2) the Army's tendency to manage officers by placing bodies in slots rather than matching skills with positions, a topic that has been discussed in some length; 3) the practice of levying school quotas that exceeded actual requirements, as many officers were consequently sent to a school only to fill a quota; 4) policy churn at the Headquarters, Department of the Army (HQDA) level; frequent changes in requirements and personnel policies disrupted career management plans and practices and added another level of complexity to the branch manager's task of aligning positions with skills and abilities; and 5) the tendency of local commanders to divert incoming officers from the jobs for which they were requisitioned and trained.[35]

The fifth point needs some elaboration. Local commanders, exercising their command prerogatives, further reduced the likelihood of effecting a job-skills-education alignment because of their focus on effectively staffing their own organization. Consequently, they made assignments that filled the command's most pressing need first; the junior officer's skills or education became a secondary consideration at best. This naturally caused disillusionment among junior officers who felt that they were not trained for the job they were performing, or they were not performing the job for which they were trained.[36]

The probability that a junior officer would stay in the Army, it was recognized, was greatest when he performed responsible and rewarding jobs. Line duties that ultimately led to command assignments offered greater intrinsic satisfaction than administrative or support duties such as motor pool officer, housing officer, or club officer. Captains who had commanded and had performed the normal progression of duties as lieutenants leading to that assignment stayed in the Army at much higher rates that those who had performed less responsible duties.[37]

Interestingly, junior officers who had served in Vietnam had, as a group, the highest tendency to remain in the Army. In fact, the retention of Reserve officers who had served in Vietnam was four times higher than those who had served only in the United States. Many of the administrative requirements of the garrison and training environments that junior officers considered to be artificial and unnecessary were waived or given a low priority in Vietnam. Moreover, the junior officer was, for the most part, utilized in his MOS and given an opportunity to command at the platoon or company level under the most challenging conditions. Many officers stated that combat tours in Vietnam had provided them with their only assignment that afforded them a challenge, responsibility with authority, independence, and a high sense of accomplishment.[38]

The Army was unable to provide a comparable degree of job satisfaction to the Vietnam veteran in stateside assignments. Large junior officer over-strengths had accumulated on Army installations in the continental United States (CONUS), especially in training centers. Many junior officers found themselves engaged in meaningless "make work" assignments or performing degrading jobs. Many who subsequently left the service stated that if they could have experienced the feeling of challenge, responsibility, independence, and achievement that they enjoyed in Vietnam, they would have stayed in the Army.[39]

To address the downward spiral in retention rates, the DCSPER asked the Franklin Institute Research Laboratories (FIRL) to conduct a study of the various factors that influenced junior officers' career decisions. The study, completed on September 30, 1968, was based on a career motivation questionnaire and personal interviews completed by 4,532 company grade officers with more than 6 months but less than 5 years' active federal commissioned service. It served as the basis for a Department of the Army (DA) plan, implemented in FY 1970 and published in DA *Pamphlet 600-20*, to improve junior officer retention. Although not all of the 44 separate actions listed in the aforementioned document can be listed or discussed, a brief overview can provide a sense of its scope and focus.[40]

First, considerable attention was given to the need to establish and sustain multiple channels of communication between junior officers and senior leaders. Career management policies and procedures and career opportunities were to be presented and explained to the junior officer throughout his initial tour of service. In addition, a block of instruction on career counseling was to be incorporated in all basic and advanced courses and training literature, and lesson plans and other publications were to be updated to address the problems of over-supervision and communications between superiors and subordinates. Another area that received considerable attention was civilian education opportunities for junior officers. In the FIRL survey, junior officers had expressed a strong desire to further their civilian education. Three specific areas were addressed: 1) the need to request more funds for civilian schooling; 2) the need to expand on-post college programs; and 3) the importance of allowing selected junior officers to attend college courses during duty hours.[41]

The need to improve fringe benefits was also recognized in the plan, although the majority of actions in this area called only for additional studies to be made. The Surgeon General, for example, was asked to study several proposals dealing with medical benefits, while the Army's chief logistician was asked to consider several proposals dealing with housing and commissary matters of particular interest to junior officers and their wives.[42]

Oddly, in light of the emphasis placed on job satisfaction, only two of the 44 actions were aimed at improving the intrinsic value of duty assignments. The two actions had as their goals the conversion of quasi-military duties to other than commissioned officer spaces and the limitation of the time that a junior officer would spend in a quasi-military billet. To achieve these goals, the plan suggested that the management of certain unconvertible quasi-military positions be entrusted to branches, which would control assignments to these billets under a specific career plan.[43]

Pay was addressed in only one of the 44 approved actions and then in a very limited way since the Hubble Pay Plan, a comprehensive military compensation package promising substantial pay raises, was then in the vetting process. Thus, the plan's proposals were restricted to issues such as commuting and dislocation expenses and housing adjustments, which were recommended for further evaluation.[44]

Finally, taking a page out of the FIRL study, the Army tried to involve senior officers more directly and more actively in retention efforts. Through DA publications and the exhortations of senior Army leaders, local commanders were to be imbued with the idea that the counseling of junior officers was one of their prime responsibilities. The assumption, based on the results of the FIRL study and other surveys, was that direct and regular communication between senior officers and lieutenants was key to persuading high quality individuals to remain in the Army.[45]

The action plan that the Army put together, as perhaps is evident from the overview presented here, was woefully insufficient. It lacked decisiveness, direction, and specificity. The wording of the approved actions allowed the widest possible latitude for interpretation and implementation at all levels of command and almost ensured that no significant results would ensue. Several of the actions, in fact, only required additional studies to be made of particular issues. Moreover, many of the most formidable obstacles to retention — the dissatisfaction flowing from frequent moves and family separations, for example — were virtually ignored or treated in the most superficial fashion.[46]

One lesson learned by Army leaders during this era was the apparent futility of targeting the well-educated for retention in the service. That is not to say, of course, that the Army rejected such individuals, only that it decided not to make extraordinary efforts to attract and retain them. Thus, instead of going all out to provide job satisfaction to its pool of highly educated lieutenants and captains, it set about to educate those officers most likely to pursue a military career — i.e., those officers without degrees and those ROTC graduates from less selective schools. To paraphrase the FIRL study, the Army had concluded that it could not motivate the highly educated but it could educate the highly motivated. Consequently, educational initiatives such as the degree completion program received a renewed emphasis in this era.[47]

The realization that the educated and affluent tended to shun a military career was not new, but it did undergo a kind of crystallization during this period. Several factors contributed to this. First, the Army in the late-1960s and early-1970s was moving toward an All-Volunteer Force and had to pay careful attention to personnel costs. The material aspirations of the less educated were easier to fulfill than those of the highly educated. Second, the company man model that informed the officer personnel management system had as one of its underlying assumptions that talent could be "grown" through a series of developmental assignments and periodic professional training. The supposition was that almost anyone, provided he or she possessed a certain minimum level of intellect and ability, could be shaped into an effective leader. Experience counted for far more than innate ability in this system. Third, by the late-1960s, a number of studies had been completed and a significant amount of data had been collected that painted a fairly clear picture of who stayed in the Army and who did not. While the studies did not constitute a holistic strategy for retention, they did establish quite conclusively that educational attainment and socioeconomic status were inversely related to the likelihood of one's pursuing a career as an Army officer. Finally, by the early-1970s, most of the senior officers who had been commissioned in the late-1930s had passed from the scene or were about to do so. Their successors, brought up in the Cold War, did not experience the interwar Army and entertained a different set of assumptions and expectations about officers and the Officer Corps.

SUMMARY AND CONCLUSION

World War II and the Cold War had altered drastically the character and composition of the Army's Officer Corps. Not only were officer requirements much greater than they had been in the interwar period, but a new set of international and domestic conditions changed the dynamics of officer accessions and retention. After 1945, the material incentives associated with a military career declined. Pay, fringe benefits, housing, medical and dental care, life insurance, and post exchange and commissary privileges all suffered significant erosion. At the same time, the prestige of being an officer fell, while the nature of the Officer Corps changed drastically. The relatively small, cohesive, and homogenous Officer Corps of the interwar era was transmogrified into the distended, mottled, and loosely integrated one of the Cold War era.

Just as significantly from the standpoint of officer retention, the nature of military jobs, along with the working conditions in which officers had to operate, changed radically after World War II. The new sense of urgency and the increased emphasis on readiness induced by the demands of the Cold War helped bring these changes about—changes that many believed dissuaded the brightest and most capable junior officers from pursuing a military career. The constant state of tension and focus on readiness that the Cold War brought to military life drove the Army toward the centralization of command, control, and training. Training was now closely supervised and tightly controlled by detailed directives and schedules. Junior officers were held on a very short leash and not allowed to exercise their judgment and originality in their work. Since there was little room for error in this environment, junior officers found themselves engaged in many routine and trivial matters that their predecessors in the interwar years had left to NCOs.

After 1945, the emergence of the Cold War with the Soviet Union forced the nation to maintain a huge active Army. To lead this greatly expanded force, the Army adopted a quantity-based rather than talent-based retention strategy. That strategy, however, had unforeseen and untoward consequences. For by accessing and retaining a large number of marginally qualified officers, it drove many of the most talented and highly educated junior officers out of the service.

The Army continued to struggle with junior officer attrition problems through the 1960s and into the 1970s. Many of the old obstacles to retention, of course, remained — although some of them in a slightly different form. Pay, benefits, housing, long hours, family separation, and frequent moves retained their salience, as did the difficulties created by the maintenance of a two-tiered Officer Corps in which OTRA captains and lieutenants (who comprised the bulk of the Officer Corps) were accorded second class status. New obstacles cropped up to add another level of complexity to the Army's attrition woes. The emergence of anti-war and anti-military attitudes, the tremendous expansion of OCS and the simultaneous erosion of accessions standards, and the creation of large junior officer over-strengths in CONUS Army installations were some of the new challenges with which senior leaders had to contend. That last condition — the large junior officer over-strengths — greatly aggravated the already huge problem that the Army was having with providing meaningful and challenging jobs to its lieutenants and captains.

Although attrition created huge shortages in the ranks of junior officers, it was the qualitative consequences of officer attrition that garnered the most concern. After 1945, the Army lost the most educated and skilled officers to civilian firms. Many voices warned of the effects that this loss of talent would eventually have on the Officer Corps in terms of both military proficiency and societal prestige.

Measures were taken to boost retention and keep the most talented junior officers in the Army. In the 25 years after the end of World War II, in fact, the problem was studied by a host of boards, commissions, agencies, and think tanks who made recommendations about how to solve it. The actions adopted by the Army to allay its retention troubles, however, were largely ineffectual, especially when it came to the qualitative aspect of the problem. The steps that the Army prescribed were incremental and generally lacked decisiveness, specificity, or long-term vision. Wide latitude for interpretation was accorded to commanders in the implementation of these actions, and many of the most complicated or difficult problems were for all practical purposes ignored. Moreover, the egalitarian ideology of the Army and its commitment to the cult of the generalist prevented it from targeting the highly or technically educated for retention. Thus, pay raises were across the board rather than the targeted variety.

By the early-1970s, a sort of consensus had emerged within the ranks of Army leaders. Instead of concentrating on attracting and retaining the highly talented and educated, it was agreed that the Army should focus on developing and educating the highly motivated. Taking extraordinary measures to attract and retain the cream of the American undergraduate population would, they concluded, lead to frustration and failure. That is not to say that the Army wanted to exclude or discourage these high academic achievers from following an Army career, only that they could not be the Army's focus. This manner of looking at retention fit the budgetary realities of an all-volunteer force and accorded closely with the assumptions that underpinned the company man system of personnel management.

Much has changed, of course, since the end of conscription in the early-1970s. The international and domestic challenges facing the United States today are much different than those encountered during that era. The Army has changed as well over the past 36 years, reconfiguring itself several times to meet evolving changing threats and demands. Still, much of the thinking that undergirded ineffectual Army officer retention policies in the 1960s and 1970s prevails today, despite fundamental changes in the American labor market. In the Army's Officer Corps, experience and motivation still count for far more than technical skills and intellectual attainment.

ENDNOTES - CHAPTER 3

1. Edward M. Coffman, *The Regulars: The American Army, 1898-1941*, Cambridge, MA: Belknap Press of Harvard University Press, 2004, pp. 147-148. In anticipation of the large Army authorized by the National Defense Act of 1920, the War Department commissioned 5,229 officers in 1920. The large number of officers in this "hump," as it would become known, combined with the practice of promotion by seniority and a mandatory retirement age of 64, created a logjam in advancement. By 1932, almost 4,200 officers — which represented roughly a third of the Officer Corps — were between the ages of 37 and 43; 1,885 captains and 234 lieutenants were in their 40s. This discouraged some from remaining in the Army. The USMA class of 1915, of which Eisenhower was a member, entered the Army before the "hump" was brought in and held relatively high rank and responsible positions during the interwar period. That class saw only 12 (or 7 percent) of its members resign before the outbreak of World War II. The USMA class of 1923, on the other hand, had to contend with both the hump and the fiscal austerity of the interwar era. It consequently lost 71 (or 24 percent) of its members to the civilian world before 1941, which was considered at the time to be a very high attrition rate. Charles J. Denholm, *Officer Promotion and Elimination*, Individual Study, Carlisle, PA: U.S. Army War College, March, 1956, p. 4.

2. J. G. Harbor, "The Army as a Career," *The Officer's Guide*, Washington, DC: National Service Publishing Company, 1930, pp. 1-19; John G. Taber, *Career Incentives for Officers*, Individual Study, Carlisle, PA: U.S. Army War College, March 1954, pp. 4-5, 8; Samuel D. Burns, *Career Incentives for Officers*, Individual Study, Carlisle, PA: U.S. Army War College, March 1954, p. 21; James B. Leer, *Career Incentives for Officers*, Individual Study, Carlisle, PA: U.S. Army War College, March 1954, p. 4; Willard Latham, *The Army as a Career*, Student Thesis, Carlisle, PA: U.S. Army War College, February 1968, p. 11; Max L. Pitney, *Retention of Junior Officers*, Student Thesis, Carlisle, PA: U.S. Army War College, March 1959, pp. 8, 12.

3. Elbridge Colby, *The Profession of Arms*, New York and London, United Kingdom (UK): D. Appleton and Company, 1924, pp. 21-22; Morris Janowitz, *The Professional Soldier*, London, UK: Times Publishing Company, Ltd., 1962, p. 65; Taber, pp. 4-5, 8; Burns, p. 21; Leer, p. 4; Latham, p. 11; Pitney, pp. 8, 12.

4. R. Earnest Dupuy, "Pass in Review," *The Army Combat Forces Journal*, Vol. 5, No. 3, October 1954, p. 48; Taber, pp. 7, 9, 14, 24; Latham, p. 12.

5. Dwight D. Eisenhower, Message from the President of the United States Relative to the Personnel Turnover in the Military Service of the United States, House of Representatives, 84th Cong., 1st Sess., January 13, 1955; "The Womble Report of Service Careers," *Army Information Digest*, February 1954, pp. 24-36; Kay L. Wieland, "Junior Officer Retention: *The Army's Dilemma*, Student Thesis, Carlisle, PA: U.S. Army War College, March 1970, p. 2; Leer, pp. 1, 2, 10; Taber, pp. 29, 31.

6. Denholm, p. 15.

7. Hanson W. Baldwin, "The Problem of Army Morale," *New York Times Magazine*, December 5, 1954, pp. 9, 55; Francis W. O'Brien, *Long Range Procurement Plan for Regular Army Officers*, Individual Study, Carlisle, PA: U.S. Army War College, March 1955, pp. ii, 19, 28, 33; Denholm, p. 16; Pitney, p. 3.

8. U.S. Congress, Senate Committee on Armed Services, Officers Grade Limitation Act of 1954, H.R. 7103, Washington, DC: U.S. Government Printing Office, 1954.

9. Hanson W. Baldwin, "What's Wrong With The Regulars," *Saturday Evening Post*, October 31, 1953, pp. 19-21, 104-110; Denholm, pp. 29, 32, 41.

10. Leer, p. 10; Denholm, pp. 1, 5-7.

11. Taber, pp. 36, 38, 47; Denholm, p. 20.

12. U.S. Department of Defense, *A Modern Concept of Manpower Management and Compensation*, Vol. 1, and *Military Personnel: Report by the Defense Advisory Committee on Professional and Technical Compensation*, Cordiner Committee, Washington, DC: May 1957, pp. 23-27; O'Brien, p. ii; Burns, p. 5; Pitney, pp. 13, 23.

13. U.S. Department of the Army, Leadership Human Research Unit (HUMRRO), *The Retention of Army Career Personnel: An Analysis of Problems and Some Proposals for Research*, Presidio of Monterey, CA, August 1958; Leer, pp. 5, 20-22; Burns, pp. 4-5; Pitney, pp. 6-7, 13, 23; Taber, pp. 31, 39. Between October 1, 1949, and May 1, 1952, for example, industrial wages rose 21 percent, while military pay increased by a mere 5.7 percent.

14. Taber, pp. 24, 31, 47; Leer, p. 30, Burns, p. 21.

15. U.S. Adjutant General's Officer, "Benefits or Improvements that Would Contribute Most toward Increasing the Value of an Army Career," Survey Prepared by Personnel Research and Procedures Division, Washington, DC, 1958; Robert H. Nevins, Jr., *The Retention of Quality Junior Officers – A Challenge for the Seventies*, Student Thesis, Carlisle, PA: U.S. Army War College, March, 1970, p. 10; Pitney, pp. ii, 13, 28-29, 37; Leer, pp. 23, 26; Taber, p. 22; Houck Spencer, *Evaluation of the Regular Officer Corps or the United States Army by Historical Professional Standards*, Student Thesis, Carlisle, PA: U.S. Army War College, March 1958, p. 6.

16. Dupuy, pp. 44-45; Denholm, p. 20; Pitney, pp. ii, 18, 23; Taber, p. 22, Leer, p. 8.

17. Willard G. Wyman, "Army Needs Captainship," *Army,* December 1957, p. 41; "Faithful to our Trust," *Combat Forces Journal,* December, 1954, pp. 18-21; U.S. Department of the Army, *What the 1956 Soldier Thinks; A Digest of Attitude and Opinion Studies,* Washington, DC: The Adjutant General's Office, 1957, p. 13.

18. Denholm, p. 16; Leer, p. 32; Pitney, pp. 8, 12, 15-16, 18, 24.

19. Pitney, p. 39.

20. Office of the Deputy Chief of Staff for Personnel, *Officer Prestige and Career Attractiveness: Resignations of Junior Regular Army Officers,* Washington, DC: U.S. Department of the Army, January 1957.

21. Wieland, p. 2.

22. *Ibid.,* p. 40.

23. *Ibid.,* pp. 2, 36.

24. Office of the Deputy Chief of Staff for Personnel, *Annual Historical Summary (AHS): FY 1966,* Washington, DC: ODCSPER, p. 40; Nevins, p. 1.

25. Nevins, pp. 1, 22.

26. Thomas H. Spence, *Job Satisfaction as a Factor in Junior Officer Recruitment and Retention,* Carlisle, PA: U.S. Army War College, March, 1972, p. 16; Wieland, pp. 27-28, 32.

27. J. W. Fulbright, "Militarism and American Democracy," *Vital Speeches of the Day,* May 15, 1969, p. 458.

28. U.S. Congress, Senate, Committee on Armed Services, *Military Pay Increase, Hearings before the Committee on HR 9075, S. 2230, S.1095,* 89th Cong., 1st Sess., 1965, p. 94; Spence, p. 5; Wieland, p. 22.

29. *Career Motivation of Army Personnel, Junior Officer Duties,* September 30, 1968, Vol. II, Boston, MA: FIRL, pp. 62-63; Nevins, p. 10.

30. Jay B. Mowray and Aaron B. Nadel, *Motivation and Retention in the U.S. Army*, Research Study 66-5, Washington, DC: U.S. Army Personnel Research Office, Chief of Research and Development, 1966, p. 20; Nevins, p. 57.

31. FIRL, Vol. II, p. 70; *Army Historical Summary, FY 1968*, ODCSPER, p. 63.

32. Nevins, p. 55.

33. U.S. Department of the Army, *Study to Compare Existing Military Environment with the Military Environment of 1937*, Washington, DC: Office of the Deputy Chief of Staff for Personnel, 1966, p. B-7; Latham, p. 37.

34. *Career Motivation of Army Personnel, Junior Officer Duties*, Vol. II, September 30, 1968, p. 619.

35. Wieland, p. 10.

36. *Ibid.*

37. Spencer, p. 12.

38. *Ibid.*, p. 14; Nevins, pp. 24.

39. Nevins, p. 72.

40. U.S. Department of the Army, *Pamphlet 600-20, Junior Officer Retention*, Washington, DC: The Adjutant General's Office, August 1969, pp. 1-6.

41. *Army Historical Summary, FY 1969*, p. 63; Wieland, p. 43.

42. Wieland, pp. 43-44.

43. *Army Historical Summary, FY 1969*, pp. 49, 63.

44. *Ibid.*, p. 63; Wieland, p. 52.

45. *Army Historical Summary, 1969*, p. 63; Wieland, pp. 46-47.

46. Wieland, pp. 46-47.

47. Nevins, p. 46; Spence, p. 16.

CHAPTER 4

ACCESSING OFFICER TALENT

INTRODUCTION

There are few issues that incite passionate discussion within the Army more than officer accessions. Source of commission is a sensitive subject that is approached with caution by most Army leaders. Indeed, this sensitivity has sometimes inhibited an honest and open discussion of some of the most elemental and critical aspects of officer accessions.

This chapter, however, steers clear of contentious comparisons between officer accessions sources, focusing instead upon the varying educational requirements and intellectual screening mechanisms that the Army has used over the last 60 years to regulate entry into the Officer Corps. The Reserve Officer Training Corps (ROTC) receives the most thorough treatment because, in the post-World War II era, it has been (except for relatively brief periods during conflicts) the largest source of Army officers. Equal attention is devoted to the Officer Candidate School (OCS) during those periods when it provided a significant volume of new officer accessions. Discussion of the U.S. Military Academy (USMA) is limited, due to its relatively low susceptibility to the fiscal pressures and forces that have caused frequent, whipsaw changes in ROTC and OCS accessions policies. This chapter begins its treatment of officer accessions in the interwar period and ends that treatment in the mid-1990s, the point at which the *Accessing Talent* monograph produced by the Office of Economic and Manpower Analysis begins its narrative.

INTERWAR PERIOD

West Point dominated officer accessions in the 2 decades before World War II. Indeed, for several years in the 1930s, the USMA provided the only input into the Officer Corps. The Army obtained a modest number of its new officers during the interwar period from "civil life," a category made up largely of graduates of civilian universities and senior military colleges. Participation by enlisted men in the commission program was negligible. The enlisted ranks accounted for less than 3 percent of the annual officer accessions cohort in the early-1920s and less than 1 percent in certain years during the 1930s.[1]

During this period, the ROTC did not produce many Active-Duty Army officers. The mission of the ROTC during this period was to produce officers for the Officers' Reserve Corps (ORC) — a manpower pool that could be drawn upon in case of mobilization. It was not until the mid-1930s that an avenue opened for ROTC graduates to serve on Active Duty, and then on a very limited basis. The Thomason Act of 1935 authorized a year of Active Duty for 1,000 ROTC graduates annually, 50 of whom could be awarded Regular Army (RA) commissions upon completion of their tours.[2]

The Army had many more applicants for commissions than it had officer vacancies during the interwar years. Since commissions were highly valued, competition for them was intense, made even more so by the onset of the Great Depression in 1929. In this environment, accessions standards were high and the candidate screening process rigorous. West Point could accept only a fraction of applicants and could therefore be fairly selective in its admissions. Men seeking commissions from "civil life" (or from the enlisted ranks) were subject to stringent physical, moral, and educational examinations. The educational examination was quite extensive and required a passing knowledge of the principal subjects covered in good undergraduate programs. Candidates for a "line" commission, for example, had to pass oral and written tests in U.S. history, geography, spelling, grammar, composition, algebra, plane geometry, natural science, and "ordinary problems involving the use of logarithms," in addition to tests required by the branch for which they were applying. Candidate review boards also screened candidates based on their ability to think clearly and express themselves in a clear and logical manner.[3]

The strict selection and screening process used by the Army promoted a high level of intellectual attainment in the Officer Corps. Between 1920 and 1940, nearly all new officers were college graduates in a time when an undergraduate degree was a true mark of distinction and a much more uncommon accomplishment than it is today.[4]

WORLD WAR II

World War II forced the Army to reconfigure its officer accessions, not in accordance with any strategic imperatives, but in response to dynamic and dangerous external conditions that the War Department tried to accommodate as best it could. The demands of the time caused frequent changes in accessions policies, and the entire officer procurement effort took on an improvised and tentative quality. Production surpluses were followed by production shortages as personnel managers attempted to regulate a very complex process that few seemed to understand in total. Despite these troubles and the unavoidable inefficiency and wastage that accompanied them, the system proved resilient and effective enough to supply the Army's officer needs in World War II.

The vast majority of officers who led an Army that eventually grew to 8,300,000 men came from three sources: 1) peacetime military training agencies — the National Guard (NG), the Officers' Reserve Corps (ORC), the ROTC, and the Citizens' Military Training Camps (CMTC); 2) the civilian community — a body of men with special skills who were awarded direct commissions and served primarily in the technical and professional services; and 3) OCS.[5]

OCS was by far the largest source of new officers during the war. In its selection of candidates, the Army, as it had in World War I, gave preference to enlisted men, since they were widely viewed as making the best platoon leaders, superior to both ROTC and West Point graduates.[6] It used the Army General Classification Test (AGCT) to screen OCS candidates. Administered to all inductees, this test purportedly measured both native abilities and talents gained via schooling and social experience. Numerical scores were grouped into five classes, with Class I representing the highest intelligence and Class V the lowest. To qualify as an officer, a man had to fall into Class I or II. Thus, the Army tried to ensure that all of its officers possessed a minimum level of intellectual attainment.[7]

To provide officers for the vastly expanded Army, however, the War Department had to make certain compromises with educational standards. Whereas before the war, line commissions had been virtually restricted to college graduates, tens of thousands of non-degreed men now flooded into the Officer Corps.

The educational "standard" prescribed in Army regulations was merely the possession of "such education or civil or military experience as will reasonably insure satisfactory completion of the course." This left a lot of room for interpretation.[8]

As the mobilization progressed, the Army had to reach deeper and deeper into its pool of enlisted talent to get OCS candidates. As one official history of the OCS program put it, Army Ground Forces (AGF) staff officers had to seek out "ways of squeezing the maximum number of graduates from the material at hand despite the fact that the supply of even poorly-qualified candidates was none too abundant." Observers at AGF headquarters noted a marked decline in the quality of new officer accessions as the war progressed.[9]

FROM WORLD WAR II TO VIETNAM

World War II transformed the Army, and nowhere was this more evident than in the Officer Corps. One of the most striking changes that took place was the drop-off in the percentage of college graduates. Before the war, over 75 percent of the Officer Corps had baccalaureate degrees. By 1955, only 49 percent did.[10]

The Army was able to maintain its authorized officer strength in the post-war years in part because of the huge influx of non-degreed officers during the war. While most officers in this category separated soon after the war's end, thousands were retained in a career status. The wartime injection of these high school graduates into the Officer Corps created a 5-year "hump" of excessive strength and reduced the number of spaces available for lieutenants and captains. The number of junior officers was further diminished by the continual cutting of new accessions to bring the Army into alignment with rapidly declining authorized strengths. As a result, the Officer Corps suffered from a severe rank imbalance. Throughout most of the 1940s and 1950s, it had many more senior and far fewer junior officers than needed.[11]

The dynamics of officer accessions changed drastically in the post-war period. After dominating the accessions process for a century and a half, West Point lost its quantitative preeminence as a commissioning source. The vast size of the Cold War defense establishment, of course, was the reason why. Indeed, by the mid-1950s, ROTC was producing more regular officers than the USMA and, by the early-1960s, was responsible for more than 80 percent of annual officer accessions. Meanwhile, OCS, drastically cut back and then discontinued for a time following World War II and was reinvigorated in 1951 due to demand stemming from the Korean conflict. Out of that experience, Army personnel managers decided to keep the program in operation to facilitate its regeneration during an emergency.[12] From the early-1950s, then, OCS remained a permanent part of the commissioning mix, producing between 6-10 percent of all active officer accessions until the Vietnam war.

The ability of the Army to screen candidates for commissioning dropped markedly after World War II as the attractiveness of an Army career plummeted. The erosion of pay and benefits, the presence of many low quality officers left over from the war, a booming economy, and the declining prestige of the military profession made military service a relatively uninviting option for the talented college graduate. The calculus of officer accessions now was very different than it had been in the interwar period. Then, the Army had a surfeit of college graduate applicants and was able to exercise great discretion in its selection process. Officers were obtained on a competitive, selective basis from what one colonel described as "a higher caliber group in our society." After 1945, however, there were fewer applicants than required. Those that the Army did attract, moreover, were, as a group, not drawn from the nation's most capable undergraduates. For all practical purposes, then, little screening took place.[13]

Even West Point, which historically had been considered the Army's "gold standard" for commissioning, struggled to fill its cadet corps with qualified applicants. Admissions standards were intermittently lowered to secure enough students. There were several years in the decade after 1945, in fact, in which USMA authorities had to invoke special provisions of the law to appoint cadets to vacancies that had gone unfilled because of the absence of a sufficient number of qualified candidates through the normal appointment system.[14]

The ROTC, too, found it difficult to enroll top notch students. One U.S. Army War College (USAWC) student at the time noted that the Army's collegiate commissioning program was filled with "lower caliber individuals" despite the fact that all were college undergraduates. Problems surfaced in the immediate aftermath of the war. At that time, the Army took note of the high rate of academic failures among ROTC cadets. Too many students were being trained in ROTC and subsequently dismissed because they did not complete the minimum requirements for a baccalaureate degree. Concerned about this trend, in May 1946, the War Department General Staff directed the Adjutant General to devise a test that would screen out those undergraduates who did not possess the ability to attain a college degree. The result was the development of the ROTC Qualifying Test 3 (RQ-3). At the same time, the ROTC Personal Inventory was introduced as an instrument to predict leadership ability and measure motivation.[15]

The RQ-3 test was first administered in 1949. Within months of its introduction, however, it was suspended because it was screening too many candidates out of the ROTC program and preventing the Army from achieving its officer production goals. The inception of the Air Force ROTC and the expansion of the Naval ROTC had intensified competition for qualified officer candidates among the services. Under these conditions, the Army felt that it had no choice but to sacrifice quality for quantity.[16]

Some argued that the ROTC's growth in the early-1950s further diluted cadet quality. This growth was fueled by several factors. The draft deferment that ROTC participation conferred upon military age youth motivated many undergraduates to enroll in the program. At the same time, the Army embarked upon a major institutional expansion of ROTC to meet the needs of the Korean war. ROTC units were eagerly sought after by college presidents, who saw them as a way to maintain or boost their institutions' enrollments and financial solvency. The convergence of these factors, coupled with the suspension of the RQ-3 qualification test, soon drove officer production well above the needs of the active Army. As a result, hundreds of minimally qualified officers received commissions. Many could not meet the minimum mental standards required for admission into OCS, and complaints arose that even Distinguished Military Graduates (DMGs), supposedly the cream of the ROTC crop, were, as a group, substandard officer material.[17]

Concerned about officer quality, the Army at the 1953 summer camps administered the RQ-3 examination to all attendees. Twenty percent of the cadets failed the test. From this and other indicators, senior Army leaders concluded that units had been given to colleges whose students did not have the potential to become officers. The schools with the highest failure rates were "in nearly every case" open admission— they required only a high school diploma for matriculation. It was noted that many of these open admission colleges were located in the South and drew their student population from small high schools with uneven standards. The academic demands placed on students attending these colleges were "correspondingly low."[18]

As a result, on September 18, 1953, the Department of the Army directed that all ROTC students must attain a score of 115 on the RQ-3 test to be admitted into the advanced course. There was general agreement that this move had a desirable effect. The requirement ensured a minimum mental capability in officer aspirants regardless of the standards of the college that they attended. Still, the Army was not satisfied with the quality of the product that ROTC was turning out. The reinstatement of the RQ-3 had reduced the worst abuses, but it did not reverse the post-war trend that saw the cream of America's undergraduates generally avoid military service, particularly service in the Army.[19]

OCS also faced difficulties during this period, although its problems were of a different nature. Throughout the 1950s, OCS had a very high average attrition rate of 44 percent. By comparison, the average rate during World War II was 33 percent. Observers blamed inadequate screening and selection mechanisms for the higher attrition. Service on OCS selection boards was an additional duty for officers; most considered such service a distraction from their principal responsibilities. Consequently, screening for motivation and suitability was often hasty and haphazard.[20]

Screening for mental ability was more systematic. OCS applicants had to attain a score of 115 on the Officer Candidate Test (OCT) for admission (the OCT was essentially equivalent to the RQ-3; both required a score of 115 to pass). Thus, the OCS selection process from 1950-54 was actually more rigorous than for ROTC. Observers found a close correlation between OCT scores and attrition rates, as individuals scoring below 115 failed the course in disproportionately high numbers. The "best candidates" scored between 126 and 155. Authorities were reluctant to increase the minimum score, however, because they recognized that it would result in an unacceptable reduction in eligible candidates.[21]

The educational requirements for acceptance into OCS, on the other hand, were minimal. To be admitted, applicants needed only a high school diploma or a general educational development (GED) certificate. Such a low educational standard, many Army leaders recognized, had a number of untoward effects. First, it lowered graduation rates at OCS; researchers found that there was a high correlation between success in the program and level of education. Second, it was a significant handicap to those marginally educated officers when they entered the field grade ranks. They found it difficult to deal with subordinates with better educations. Third, it had a deleterious effect on the quality of the Officer Corps as a whole. The example set by these minimally educated officers discouraged the most capable lieutenants and junior captains from staying in the service.[22]

One of the persistent problems faced by the Army in the 1940s and the 1950s was its inability to convince large numbers of men to apply for officer candidate training. While OCS was expanding in World War II, the demands of troop units being activated outran the supply of inductees. Serious shortages of enlisted personnel ensued. Procurement of officer candidates in the requisite numbers was therefore difficult in the extreme. The AGF felt that the trouble lay in the reluctance of unit commanders to send key men to OCS. That headquarters therefore imposed OCS quotas on all units, practically eliminating the voluntary nature of the program. The requisite quantity of officers was produced but only with difficulty and the use of rather severe methods.[23]

During the Korean war, the lack of qualified applicants again plagued the OCS program. In 1952, this led to the failure of OCS to make its officer quota. In 1953, the Army, concerned about OCS production problems, conducted a study that found that less than a third of the men eligible for OCS actually applied. After the war, things deteriorated even further. Throughout the remainder of the 1950s, in fact, only 10 percent of eligible soldiers applied for OCS. This was a major concern for Army leaders since they were convinced that the quality of officers produced depended primarily on the degree of selectivity that could be exercised in the choice of applicants.[24]

The three biggest deterrents to OCS participation, the Army found, were 1) the longer period of duty required of officers (as compared to enlisted men), 2) a belief that OCS entailed a greater likelihood of recall after separation from Active Duty, and 3) a reluctance to assume "responsibilities" (since most had no intention of staying in the service to retirement). The first deterrent listed—the longer period of obligated service—was perhaps the most important one. The more ambitious and educated enlisted men, the Army found, generally had attractive opportunities in the civilian world and consequently severed their connection with the Army as soon as they could.[25]

VIETNAM

The Vietnam war created a new accessions environment and a need for a vastly expanded Officer Corps. All three principal accessions sources saw their output substantially increased. From the onset of the Vietnam build-up, the Army wanted the ROTC to provide the bulk of its officers. However, because of the lag time associated with the ROTC commissioning process, it took the Army 4 years to ramp up ROTC production to anything approaching the desired volume. As a result, the rise in OCS production was initially most dramatic, although the Army's other pre-commissioning programs also registered historic gains.

The Department of the Army ordered a major build-up of the OCS program in August 1965. By 1967, OCS had become the Army's largest producer of officers. The 19,226 Active-Duty officers it produced that year represented the summit of post-World War II OCS production, almost twice that of the ROTC and 34 times that of West Point.[26] In 1968, however, the Army began to "phase down" the OCS program, and after that year, OCS production fell off sharply. By the early-1970s, OCS's commissioning share was back within historic norms.[27]

The Army's 1960s expansion of the ROTC actually preceded the Vietnam build-up. The John Kennedy administration had adopted a new "flexible response" strategy that entailed a significant growth in Army end strength. This only aggravated the Army's officer procurement problems, already fairly serious in the 1950s. In 1963, the Department of Defense (DoD) reported that the Army missed its annual officer accessions mission by over 2,000 lieutenants. It also suffered from qualitative shortfalls in its new officers. To be sure, due primarily to the ROTC, the percentage of college graduates in the Officer Corps had increased since the early-1950s — rising from under 50 percent to over 70 percent. Still, congressional and Army leaders were not satisfied with the caliber of officer they were getting, and all publicly acknowledged that the ground forces were not getting a fair share of the nation's talented undergraduates.[28]

To boost both the quantity and quality of officer production, Congress passed the ROTC Vitalization Act of 1964. This legislation instituted an Army ROTC scholarship program, increased the ROTC stipend, provided for a 2-year ROTC commissioning program, and expanded the Junior ROTC. After the war began, additional legislation expanded the Army ROTC from 243 units in 1964 to 285 units in 1971.[29] As a result, by 1969, ROTC had resumed its place as the Army's largest commissioning source, and reached its historic production high of over 16,000 officers in 1970.[30]

West Point also experienced growth in the 1960s. Legislation passed in 1964 raised the enrollment ceiling at the USMA from 2,500 to 4,400 cadets. As a result of this increase, the institution's officer production rose by nearly 90 percent between 1963 and 1973. As was the case with the ROTC, the legislation providing for the expansion of the USMA predated the Vietnam war. It was inspired by the same forces and qualitative and quantitative concerns about officer production that had informed the ROTC Vitalization Act of 1964.[31]

As had occurred in previous conflicts, however, much of the increase in quantity was realized at the expense of quality. Due to the pressure of numbers, the Army's ability to screen was soon restricted. All of the major accessions sources were eventually forced to lower their commissioning standards during this era.

In the case of OCS, attempts were initially made to hold the line on quality and avoid some of the turmoil that followed the expansion of the OCS program in World War II and Korea. As we have seen, before Vietnam, OCS had primarily been an avenue for enlisted people to gain a commission. In 1964, only 28 percent of the 1,688 OCS graduates commissioned that year had a college degree. The next year, the Army began to target aggressively college graduates for its OCS program. By the early-1970s, about 70 percent of OCS graduates held a baccalaureate degree. By that time, however, the annual OCS cohort had been drastically reduced from its peak in 1967. Thus, despite the Army's push to make maximum use of the OCS college graduate enlistment option, approximately half of all captains in 1970 did not have a baccalaureate degree.[32]

According to contemporary records, there were other troubling aspects of the OCS program. Some insisted that greatly diminished attrition rates were evidence of a dilution of OCS commissioning standards rather than improved candidate screening and selection. From the high average attrition rates of 44 percent that predominated throughout the late-1950s and early-1960s, in 1966, the first full year of the OCS build up for Vietnam, the rate fell to 30 percent. The next year, it sank to 20 percent. (Only after ROTC officer production reached desired levels did OCS attrition rates start rising again). Pressed for officers to meet the leadership demands of the Vietnam war, some contended the Army had no choice but to relax its screening procedures.[33]

West Point was by no means immune from the noxious effects of officer production pressures. Its ability to be selective in admissions also deteriorated as the Vietnam war dragged on. For several years in the early-1970s, in fact, the Academy had to admit virtually all minimally qualified candidates to make its numbers.

The ability of the ROTC program to cull the marginally capable from its ranks also declined, especially during the latter stages of the Vietnam war. Many factors in addition to the vastly expanded demands of the war contributed to this development. Campus and social unrest, the progressive elimination of compulsory ROTC (70 percent of ROTC units were compulsory in 1959; only 7 percent were by 1973), and the gradual lessening of draft pressures after 1969 all, it was believed, reduced ROTC enrollment and consequently reduced the Army's ability to screen officer aspirants.[34]

One method that the Army used to boost officer output through ROTC was to lower commissioning standards for students enrolled in Military Junior Colleges (MJCs). In 1966, the Deputy Chief of Staff for Personnel (DCSPER) introduced the Early Commissioning Program (ECP). The ECP permitted MJC graduates, who heretofore had to wait until they completed their baccalaureate degree to be commissioned, to enter the Officer Corps immediately upon completion of their junior college studies. Thus, instead of getting 21-year-old men with baccalaureate degrees, the Army annually commissioned several hundred 19-year-olds with associate degrees.[35]

Drastic change in the ROTC host university and college base was another factor that affected officer production. In an attempt to counter the elimination of compulsory programs and to ensure that production capacity kept pace with the officer requirements, the Army expanded ROTC by over 17 percent (from 243 to 285 colleges and universities) between 1964 and 1972. In the same timeframe, a number of universities, including Yale, Harvard, Dartmouth, and Stanford, severed their connections with the Army ROTC. Thus, in addition to the 42 schools needed to reach the 285 mark, the schools leaving the program also had to be replaced. Most of the newcomers were not top tier schools but were small or medium-sized state institutions located in the South, the Midwest, or the West.[36] This trend raised concerns about product quality, with some worrying that it would lower the intellectual level of the Officer Corps. As General Donn Starry later observed, "There is no way to replace a Harvard . . . or Yale except with Harvard or Yale."[37]

The Army used the ROTC institutional expansion to achieve greater ethnic diversity in its new officer accessions. Before World War II, most black Reserve officers received their commissions through ROTC programs at Wilberforce and Howard University. In the immediate post-war period, an additional 12 ROTC units were established at historically black colleges and universities (HBCUs) by 1949. There matters stood, and by the 1960s, African American representation in the junior officer ranks was in decline (from roughly 3 percent in 1962 to about 1.5 percent in 1969). The Army attempted to redress this by increasing its presence at HBCUs, as a high proportion of serving black Army officers had graduated from these institutions. By 1973, the number of historically black schools hosting ROTC units had risen to 19.[38]

The addition of these black colleges to its institutional portfolio brought quick ROTC enrollment and production dividends in relative, if not absolute, terms. The percentage of black graduates in the ROTC commissioning class rose from 2.6 percent in 1969 to 3.6 percent in 1973. Over the same period, the African American share of total ROTC enrollment grew from 6.6 percent to 10.8 percent.[39] These numbers seemed to bode well for the Army's diversity efforts.[40] Yet the reliance upon HBCUs had its troubling aspects. While ROTC enrollment rates at black colleges were above average, black student participation in ROTC at predominantly white institutions was well below average. This was a source of concern because in the late-1960s and early-1970s, black students in increasing numbers and percentages were attending predominantly white colleges. Additionally, ROTC units at HBCUs were much more inefficient officer producers, on average, than were units on other campuses, with far lower ratios of "cadets enrolled" to "cadets commissioned."

One reason for this inefficiency was the difficulty that HBCU-affiliated units had in qualifying their cadets for the ROTC advanced course due to years of unequal educational opportunity in the United States. In 1969, almost 49 percent of the students taking the ROTC qualification test at seven black institutions failed it, while the national failure rate was about 15.1 percent. To redress this, the Army sponsored special remedial academic programs at HBCUs to lower the failure rate among cadets. It was quite evident, however, that much more had to be done in this area if the Army hoped to realize its minority procurement goals.[41] Thus, to increase officer accessions, the Army adopted a policy of liberal waivers for scores on the RQ-8 and RQ-9 exams, the latest successors to the RQ-3 exam introduced by the Army in 1949. The minimum raw score on the RQ-8 and RQ-9 was 50. Local commanders had the authority to grant waivers for RQ scores of between 44 and 50. Continental Army Command (CONARC) headquarters was the approval authority for scores below 44.[42]

Waivers for the RQ test, along with waivers for medical, behavioral, and physical issues, started to be dispensed liberally. This helped to increase the number of minority officers attaining commissions as well as assisted the Army to maintain a certain level of officer production, as it was being gradually weaned away from the draft. It also, of course, lowered the level of intellectual attainment among junior officers.[43]

THE ADVENT OF THE ALL-VOLUNTEER FORCE

ROTC emerged from the Vietnam war as the Army's largest commissioning source. It accounted for about 75 percent of active Army accessions in the 1970s. The USMA also assumed an enhanced role relative to the one it had in the decade before Vietnam, producing 17 percent of new officers in the decade after the war. After the experience of Vietnam, with its large influx of lieutenants without degrees and the shock of the My Lai episode, the Army had become somewhat wary of officers without baccalaureate degrees.[44] OCS was therefore reduced to a "caretaker status," just large enough to ensure that it could be reactivated quickly in the event of an emergency. Its post-Vietnam share of the annual commissioning cohort averaged a modest 8 percent.

With the advent of the All-Volunteer Force (AVF), females and minorities assumed a much larger role in the Army's officer accessions plan. By the end of the 1970s, African-Americans comprised over 10 percent and women over 15 percent of the annual ROTC commissioning cohort. Women began to enter commissioning programs in large numbers in the early-1970s. After admitting them on an experimental basis in the fall of 1972, the ROTC was thrown open to women in 1973. West Point admitted its first cohort of 119 women in 1976, the same year that OCS adopted a gender integrated approach to officer training.[45]

The early- and mid-1970s were years of ambiguity in officer accessions. Due to constantly declining endstrengths, a new and enhanced role for the reserve components, and an indeterminate international situation (the first half of the 1970s were the years of détente with the Soviet Union), there was a great deal of uncertainty about what should be officer production levels. The Army's Deputy Chief of Staff for Personnel (DCSPER) noted in his annual historical summary for 1973 that the balancing of qualitative new procurement against the reductions in the force presented major problems. In fact, the ROTC operated without a definite mission through the mid-1970s. ROTC administrators were told simply to produce as many lieutenants as possible. This methodology presented no immediate problems. The Army merely took what it needed for active Army requirements and gave the remainder to the reserve components, which in the immediate aftermath of Vietnam were still brimming with officers. Only in 1976, after U.S.-Soviet relations began to worsen and reserve component officer strength approached dangerously low levels, did the Army assign a definite production objective to the ROTC.[46]

Concerns about officer accessions quality plagued the Army throughout the first decade of the AVF. With the phasing out of conscription after 1970, the Army found that it could not meet minimum Active-Duty commissioning targets without lowering accessions standards. Finding the RQ test too restrictive, it began experimenting with other tests that promised easier access into the Officer Corps. The Cadet Evaluation Battery (CEB) was selected to replace the RQ examinations. It came into widespread use in 1971. The CEB was much less rigorous than its predecessors.

Despite this relaxation of rigor, the new screening tool soon revealed a disturbing trend. Average scores on the CEB steadily declined after 1971. In that year, the average CEB score was 22. By 1975, it had dropped to 17. Some ROTC instructors claimed that the situation was worse than the test scores indicated. According to them, there were widespread irregularities in the administration of the new test. Since ROTC cadre members had total control over testing, they could provide close and detailed "coaching" to their charges. Pressed to make numbers, many of them reportedly did so.[47]

Several studies conducted during this period added to the Army's concerns about the quality of its officer aspirants. J. J. Card and W. M. Shanner of the Army Research Institute for Behavioral and Social Sciences (ARI) authored a 1976 study indicating that ROTC cadets had lower high school and college grade point averages and lower verbal aptitudes than their non-ROTC classmates. The epochal *Review of Education and Training for Officers* (RETO) study (1978), commissioned by the Chief of Staff of the Army, also expressed strong reservations about ROTC's selection methods, concluding that its "intelligence standards" were "inadequate" and suggesting that little screening and culling was being done at all.[48]

The changing character of the ROTC cadet corps was yet another source of concern. In the 1970s, the percentage of ROTC cadets attending the nation's most prestigious colleges and universities plummeted, while those enrolled at less selective institutions shot up sharply. The U.S. Army Training and Doctrine Command (TRADOC) was concerned about this trend but, given the fiscal realities of the late-1970s, the intense pressure to meet officer accessions objectives, and the relatively high employment rate that prevailed at the time, could do little to reverse it.

The Army's officer production problem became more immediate in 1976 when the DCSPER determined that, in order to meet mobilization requirements, ROTC had to produce more than 10,000 officers a year by 1980. To ramp up to this level, the Army took a number of extraordinary measures. The most controversial was the extension of the Early Commissioning Program (ECP). Previously, the ECP was available only to graduates of military junior colleges. Beginning in 1978, however, it was extended throughout the ROTC institutional base. Cadets could now receive reserve commissions through ROTC without completing a baccalaureate degree. By the early-1980s, the ECP accounted for roughly half of all ROTC commissions. Even more worrisome to Army personnel managers was the fact that there were no minimum academic standards in place to cull unqualified ECP cadets from the ranks. Students with grade point averages (GPAs) below 2.0 could now be commissioned, as scores of them were. With the ECP offering an easy road to commissioning, many officer aspirants reportedly entered the ROTC program with no intention of finishing their degree.[49]

Worries about the lack of ROTC screening and culling mechanisms deepened at the end of the 1970s, as increasing numbers of ROTC graduates began to fail their Army branch basic courses. In 1981, TRADOC Commander General Donn Starry observed:

> While we have always been concerned with ROTC graduates who perform poorly at the OBCs [Basic Officers Courses], it has been only in the past few years that this problem has become critical. Whereas in the sixties and early seventies the bottom 5 to 10 percent of ROTC graduates were fully able to complete OBC and meet minimum levels of proficiency, in recent years . . . this group is often able to accomplish neither.[50]

While a disproportionate number of the lieutenants who failed OBC came from HBCUs, the problem was widespread. Many lieutenants from ROTC's less selective, predominantly white colleges also could not meet the intellectual demands placed on them in their branch schools.

THE RONALD REAGAN ERA

The commissioning source mix in the 1980s differed little from the previous decade. ROTC's annual contribution declined slightly (from 75 to 72 percent) as did the USMA's (from 17 to about 16 percent) while OCS rose slightly (from 10 to 13 percent). The officer accessions environment in the 1980s (especially in the early part of the decade), however, was much more propitious than it had been for years. A high unemployment rate, a resurgence of patriotism, the heating up of the Cold War with the Soviet Union, and the Reagan administration's firm support of the military services helped create this environment. The Reagan administration doubled the number of ROTC's scholarships and greatly expanded its institutional base. Simultaneously, West Point became one of America's "hottest" undergraduate destinations.[51]

With high unemployment rates and more scholarships, the number and percentage of ROTC cadets enrolled in America's more selective schools mushroomed, but the gains were widespread as well. Across the program's host colleges and universities, ROTC units now enjoyed an abundance of candidates and could be more discriminating in who they commissioned. The number of waivers granted for medical, moral, and academic issues was substantially cut back, and failures of OBC gradually ceased to be a major problem.

The Army took a number of steps to increase the rigor of its officer applicant screening process. The most momentous was the introduction of the ROTC Quality Assurance System (QAS), which was designed to raise minimum contracting and commissioning standards. QAS required a minimum GPA of 2.0 for commissioning and also introduced the Officer Selection Battery (OSB) as a motivational and intellectual screening mechanism. While not as challenging as the old RQ exam, the OSB represented a modest upgrade over the CEB, which by the early-1980s had fallen into disuse.[52]

THE POST-COLD WAR ERA

The end of the Cold War ushered in a new officer accessions era. The Army had to adjust to both an ambiguous threat environment and sharp reductions in its end strength and force structure. During this period of reduced officer requirements, West Point's fixed officer production necessarily represented a larger share of annual commissions, almost 25 percent. ROTC and OCS, on the other hand, saw their share of annual commissions decline to about 67 percent and 8 percent, respectively.

The biggest officer accessions changes occurred in the ROTC program, which saw its mission significantly reduced; its institutional base, management infrastructure, and manpower cut; and its scholarship budget come under sustained attack. Fully funded scholarships were an early casualty of the post-Cold War drawdown. A cap of 80 percent of tuition was placed on scholarships in 1988, even before the fall of the Berlin Wall in Germany. Further adjustments were made to the scholarship program in the mid-1990s with the introduction of the tiered-scholarship program, which set limits on scholarship outlays and was generally successful in holding down costs, primarily because it strictly limited the ROTC footprint at top tier schools.[53]

With diminished demand, personnel managers reasoned, the Army could be more selective in who it admitted into the Officer Corps. Indeed, for a few years, this was the case. Early commissioning was virtually eliminated in 1991, with only cadets at MJCs remaining eligible. ROTC program managers became more selective in who they sent to Advanced Camp. In 1991 and 1992, many professors of military science refused to send any cadets to summer training who, in their estimation, would not excel. During those same years, Cadet Command waged an aggressive campaign to reduce the number of lateral entry cadets into the ROTC Advanced Course (students who, for the most part, entered the ROTC program as college juniors). This was because students who entered the ROTC as freshman outscored their lateral entry fellows in almost every measure of performance and aptitude.[54]

The favorable constellation of circumstances that permitted this selectivity, however, did not last. After 1992, the ROTC struggled to attract a sufficient number of qualified candidates to meet its mission. In fact, between 1992 and 2000, Cadet Command did not realize its assigned production objectives. A booming economy, low unemployment rates, and a steadily declining propensity for military service among military-aged youth made officer recruiting difficult. In response, the Army again relaxed or eliminated many ROTC screening and culling mechanisms. The number of waivers granted to cadets, for example, steadily rose. In 1986, only 3 percent of the ROTC commissioning class had waivers. Seventeen years later, over 20 percent did. By 1996, Cadet Command had also done away with the OSB. Henceforth, the ROTC operated without a standard instrument to screen for mental capacity or career motivation. OSB's demise was an admission that, in the competitive labor market of the late-1990s, the Army saw little choice but to remove qualitative barriers to officer accessions, even though those barriers might not be particularly high.[55]

Thus, by the mid-1990s, things had come full circle. The Army found itself in an accessions environment that was, in certain ways, analogous to the one that it had experienced in the early-1950s when its OCS program had more rigorous screening mechanisms in place than the ROTC. As in the early-1950s, some observers in the 1990s saw a decline in officer "quality" resulting from the absence of such screening. They feared that graduates of less competitive colleges who exhibited lower levels of intellectual attainment would come to comprise a disproportionately large portion of the Officer Corps.

CONCLUSION

During the 20th century, the general trend was for the Army to dilute or discard its culling and screening tools for its officer aspirants. The interwar years saw the Army employing rather rigorous officer selection instruments. Candidates from civil life (and the enlisted ranks) were required to pass a challenging examination that encompassed a wide range of academic subjects, as well as satisfy a board of officers as to their ability to think and express themselves clearly. Almost all new officer accessions in the 1920s and 1930s, decades when a baccalaureate degree was a mark of distinction, were college graduates. The deplorable state of the economy, the small size of the Officer Corps, and the low demand for new lieutenants permitted selectivity.

During World War II, however, intellectual standards were relaxed to meet officer requirements for an eight million-man Army. The War Department commissioned thousands of high school graduates and, as the war progressed, reached deeper into its pool of enlisted talent to come up with enough lieutenants to man the force.

The demand for vast numbers of junior officers during the Cold War did not allow for a return to the rigorous officer candidate screening of the interwar years. Lagging pay, the diminished prestige of the military profession, a booming civilian economy, and the rather turbulent internal condition of the post-war Army discouraged the nation's top tier collegians from entering the Army. Both the USMA and ROTC experienced difficulties in attracting suitable candidates.

In the immediate post-war period, the ROTC operated without an intellectual screening tool. As the Korean war wound down, however, Army leaders became concerned about the lack of such an instrument. In 1953, ROTC program managers administered the RQ-3 test to cadets at Advanced Camp and found that a fifth of them could not meet the mental standards for admission to OCS. Authorities attributed the large number of failures in part to the recent expansion of ROTC in which a number of "marginal" colleges with open admission standards were admitted into the program's institutional base. The RQ-3 exam was subsequently reinstated to ensure a minimum level of mental attainment in all new officer accessions.

Although OCS throughout the 1950s screened for mental capacity, its lower educational standards were a source of concern. To be admitted to OCS during this era, a candidate required only a high school diploma or GED certificate. Although Army personnel officers wanted to raise these standards, a lack of applicants prevented them from doing so.

The Vietnam war further strained the Army's ability to be selective about entry into commissioning programs. OCS admitted thousands of non-college educated candidates to meet wartime demands. Consequently, by 1970, half of all captains did not have a college degree. As draft pressures eased after 1969, ROTC and West Point also became less discriminating in their selection of candidates. In the early-1970s, West Point had to admit virtually all qualified candidates. ROTC relied on the liberal dispensation of waivers to meet its assigned production objectives. The RQ tests, which had ensured a minimum level of intellectual attainment in new lieutenants, were, in effect, suspended in many portions of ROTC's institutional base.

With the end of conscription, the Army made its intellectual screening mechanisms less restrictive to help meet officer production goals and diversity objectives. The CEB, which came into widespread use in the early-1970s, was less rigorous than its predecessor. Even so, CEB scores steadily declined throughout the 1970s. By the end of that decade, officer accessions had reached what some considered a crisis state. ROTC graduates, who made up three-fourths of all new officer accessions during this period, were failing their OBC in disturbingly large numbers, and there were widespread complaints within the Army's school system about the poor "quality" of many recently commissioned officers.

The recession of the early-1980s and the resurgence of patriotism that accompanied the Reagan era allowed the Army to raise accessions standards. The OSB was introduced to screen for mental capacity and career motivation, and the Quality Assurance System was developed to ensure all ROTC met minimum academic standards. This interlude of relatively high selectivity in officer accessions proved to be temporary, however. With the end of the Cold War and the decline in service propensity among college-aged youth, standards and screening were once again relaxed. In

1996, a milestone was reached when the Army discontinued use of the OSB in ROTC. Since then, the Army's largest commissioning source has operated without an intellectual screening tool. Thus, from 1945 to 2000, the Army found it increasingly difficult to screen for the talent it needs and still meet officer production and diversity objectives. Although Army accessions have been more selective during certain times (most notably during periods of high unemployment), these have been short-lived.

ENDNOTES - CHAPTER 4

1. Charles J. Denholm, *Officer Promotion and Elimination*, Individual Study, Carlisle, PA: U.S. Army War College, March, 1956, p. 8; J. G. Harbor, "The Army as a Career," *The Officer's Guide*, Washington, DC: National Service Publishing Company, 1930, p. 17.

2. Arthur T. Coumbe and Lee S. Harford, *U.S. Army Cadet Command: The 10 Year History*, Washington, DC: Government Printing Office, 1996, p. 21. Only a relative handful of ROTC graduates managed to win RA commissions. The Marine Corps took advantage of this situation and actually made greater use of Army ROTC as a source of Active-Duty commissions than the Army.

3. *Special Regulations A: Examinations of Candidates for Appointment in Regular Army*, Washington, DC: War Department, May 17, 1920, pp. 9-10; Denholm, p. 4.

4. Samuel D. Burns, *Career Incentives for Officers*, Individual Study, Carlisle, PA: U.S. Army War College, March 1954, p. 21; James B. Leer, *Career Incentives for Officers*, Individual Study, Carlisle, PA: U.S. Army War College, March 1954, p. 4.

5. R. R. Palmer, *The Procurement and Training of Ground Combat Troops*, Washington, DC: U.S. Army Center of Military History, 1948, p. 38.

6. Forrest C. Pogue, *George C. Marshall: Ordeal and Hope, 1939-1942*, New York: Viking Press, 1974, p. 97. At the beginning of mobilization, Secretary of War Henry Stimson tried to make OCS a course for college men, but General George Marshall adamantly resisted, eventually threatening resignation over the matter. In the face of this threat, the secretary yielded and let Marshall have his way.

7. Palmer, p. 103.

8. William R. Keast, *Training of Officer Candidates in AGF Special Training Schools*, Study No. 31, Washington, DC: Historical Section, Army Ground Forces, U.S. War Department, 1946, p. 53.

9. *Ibid.*, p. 18.

10. Max L. Pitney, "Retention of Junior Officers," Student Thesis, Carlisle, PA: U.S. Army War College, March, 1959, p. 12.

11. Denholm, p. 15.

12. Henry Koepcke, *A Successful Infantry OCS Program*, Student Thesis, Carlisle, PA: U.S. Army War College, March 1958, p. 11. To ramp up OCS for Korea, Army schools found that they had to develop their OCS methods and procedures almost as though the program had never existed.

13. Denholm, p. 19.

14. Coy L. Curtis, *The Selection and Development of Officers*, Student Thesis, Carlisle, PA: U.S. Army War College, March 1956, p. 40.

15. Thomas R. Bruce, *Long Range ROTC Policy*, Student Thesis, Carlisle, PA: U.S. Army War College, March, 1955, p. 31.

16. *Ibid.*, p. 25.

17. *Ibid.*, p. 26.

18. *Ibid.*, p. 30.

19. *Ibid.,* p. 26.

20. Koepcke, p. 17.

21. *Ibid.,* p. 29.

22. Report, Army Field Forces, Officer Candidate School Board, Fort Monroe, VA, February 8, 1952.

23. Koepcke, p. 32.

24. *Ibid.,* p. 35.

25. *Ibid.*

26. U.S. Army, Deputy Chief of Staff for Personnel, DSCPER, *Annual Historical Report: FY 1967,* Washington, DC, Office of the DCSPER, 1967, p. 27.

27. DCSPER, *Annual Historical Reports for FY 1968,* p. 34; FY 1969, p. 12; and FY 1970, p. 38.

28. Coumbe and Harford, p. 14.

29. *Ibid.,* p. 18.

30. DCSPER, *Annual Historical Report: FY 1969,* p. 29. The ROTC Vitalization Act of 1964 also instituted a scholarship program for the Air Force ROTC. The Naval ROTC had had such a program since 1946.

31. DCSPER, *Annual Historical Reports, FY 1963 through FY 1970,* p. 27.

32. U.S. Department of the Army, Deputy Chief of Staff for Personnel, Memorandum (DSCPER-CSD), Subject: Quality of the Officer Corps, 19 August 1964; Staff Study, Major General Frank W. Norris, *Review of Army Officer Educational System, Vol. I: Summary Report,* Washington, DC: Department of the Army, December 1, 1971, p. 7.

33. Koepcke, p. 18; DCSPER, *Annual Historical Reports for FY 1967*, p. 37; and *FY 1968*, p. 16.

34. Victor Bruce Hirshauer, "The History of the Army Reserve Officers' Training Corps, 1916-1973," Ph.D. dissertation, Baltimore, MD: Johns Hopkins University, 1975, p. 398.

35. DCSPER, *Annual Historical Report: FY 1966*, p. 41.

36. Deputy Chief of Staff for Individual Training (DCSIT, HQ), *Semiannual Historical Report, 1 January--30 June 1971*, Washington, DC: U.S. Continental Army Command (CONARC), pp. 1-2.

37. Lewis Sorley, ed., *Press On: Selected Works of General Donn A. Starry*, Fort Leavenworth, KS: Combat Institute Press, 2009, Vol. I, p. 604.

38. Clarence A. Miller, *Procurement and Retention of Black Officers*, Research Paper, Carlisle, PA: U.S. Army War College, April 1972, p. 38.

39. Robert L. Goldich, *The Senior Reserve Officer Training Corps: Recent Trends and Current Status*, Washington, DC: Congressional Research Service, April 19, 1974, p. 31.

40. Miller, p. 39; Goldich, p. 32.

41. Miller, p. 42.

42. *Ibid.*, p. 50.

43. DCSIT, U.S. CONARC, Report of the Tenth Annual CONARC ROTC Conference, September 13-14, 1972, pp. 23, 130.

44. Coumbe and Harford, p. 22.

45. *Ibid.*

46. Donald Lloyd Cummings, "Army ROTC: A Study of the Army's Primary Officer Procurement Program, 1862-1977," Ph.D. dissertation, Santa Barbara, CA: University of California, 1982, p. 118.

47. Sorley, pp. 604-605.

48. J. J. Card and W. M. Shanner, *Development of a ROTC/Army Career Commitment Model: Management Summary Report*, Palo Alto, CA: American Institute for Research, March 1976, p. 30; Department of the Army, Office of the Chief of Staff, *A Review of Education and Training for Officers* (RETO), Washington, DC: May 1986, pp. I:2, III:2.

49. Coumbe and Harford, p. 37.

50. Sorley, p. 604.

51. Coumbe and Harford, p. 58.

52. *Reserve Officers' Training Corps Study Group Report*, Washington, DC: Headquarters, Department of the Army, May 1986, p. 1-5.

53. Coumbe and Harford, p. 198.

54. Memorandum, Subject: Curtailment of Early Commissioning Program (ECP), Air Traffic Control Center-Pennsylvania (ATCC-PA)-PA, Major General Wallace C. Arnold, to DCSPER, December 6, 1990; *Cadet Command Regulation 145-9, Reserve Officers' Training Corps Accessioning and Commissioning*, Carbondale, IL: Southern Illinois University, August 24, 1992, p. 14.

55. U.S. Army Cadet Command, Briefing Slides, ATCC-MO, n.d., "Reengineering Cadet Command Alternatives," Carbondale, IL: Southern Illinois University.

CHAPTER 5

DEVELOPING OFFICER TALENT

INTRODUCTION

Since the beginning of the last century, officer development in the U.S. Army has been predicated on a combination of education, training, and experience. It has entailed formal schooling, rotation through varied assignments, service at progressively higher echelons of command, and self-study to improve overall professional capacity. Career paths (tied to job performance, longevity of service, and promotion patterns) have been structured to broaden the interests, abilities, and aptitudes of officers to enable them to function effectively in positions of steadily escalating responsibility. The mentoring of subordinates and regular performance appraisals have been, at least in theory, intrinsic elements of this developmental process. This methodology is broadly similar to that devised by the Prussians in the mid-19th century to manage modern, industrialized warfare and that used by many business firms in the industrial age.

This chapter explores two aspects of the officer development process — the Army's school system and fully funded civilian graduate education. Examining the historical evolution of these two elements highlights some of the critical and contentious issues that have surrounded officer education and training over the years and provides valuable insights into the officer development process.

THE ARMY SCHOOL SYSTEM BEFORE THE WORLD WARS

The prototype of the modern American officer development system arose in the early-20th century under Elihu Root, Secretary of War from 1899 to 1904. Root's formula for officer development was loosely based on the Prussian model, which had been the first to adapt fully the modern industrial management techniques to the conduct of warfare. This model entailed, among other things, the rotation of duty assignments and intermittent periods of professional schooling.

The professional education schema envisaged by Root necessitated an extensive makeover of the Army school network. The Secretary of War purposed to transform the existing system of isolated and disconnected military training institutions into an integrated network of schools designed to prepare officers for service as they progressed up the ranks. His was a progressive and sequential model that taught subjects and techniques targeted at specific command levels. Under this concept of professional military education, officers would attend post schools, branch schools, the staff school, and then the war college — with the stints at these schools being interspersed with periods of regular duty. At each level of education, selection based on previous achievements would reduce the number of officers attending each course. This supposedly ensured that only the most qualified and capable officers reached the apex of the educational system. With this arrangement, Root hoped to fill in many of the obvious gaps in the officer professional education system that had so hobbled the development of officers in the 19th century and that had proven so defective during the recent war with Spain.[1]

With his new educational system, Root also hoped to address the needs of the hundreds of men that had been issued emergency commissions during the war — men taken directly from civil life, promoted from the ranks, or accessed into the Officer Corps from the volunteers. These incompletely trained officers needed systematic instruction not only to fit them for service in the grades to which they had been appointed, but also to develop the capacity of each with a view to service in the higher ranks.[2]

At the base of the professional education edifice constructed by Root was the garrison school. Previously, the post lyceum, or local study organization, was used as the chief pedagogical means for instructing junior officers in leadership and basic professional military skills. Under Root, this system of local lectures and classes was upgraded and expanded into garrison schools at all posts with at least four companies assigned. The instruction presented at these garrison schools was controlled by the War Department and was intended to prepare the junior officer for attendance at the various branch schools then being erected.

Branch schools, which formed the next rung of the educational pyramid, underwent a significant expansion and upgrade under Root. In the decade after 1901, schools for the ordnance and quartermaster corps were created, while the schools for the engineers, signal corps, artillery, and infantry were extensively overhauled and, in some cases, expanded. Technological innovation also drove the expansion of the school system. Probably the best example of this is the School for Submarine Defense opened at Fort Totten, NY, in 1901.[3]

In 1902, the former "School of Application for Infantry and Cavalry" re-emerged in Root's system as the "General Service and Staff School." The Fort Leavenworth, KS, school was designed as a combined staff school at an educational level above the branch schools. Its focus was on preparing its charges for high level command and staff responsibilities. In fact, the school's declared purpose was to prepare its students for effective service at divisional, corps, and army headquarters.[4]

Students who attended the course were generally captains who had completed their branch school. Merit selection rather than competitive examinations determined attendance eligibility. Then, as today, performance on the job counted for more that intellectual accomplishment in determining who would reap the benefits of professional military education.[5]

At the top of the Army school pyramid constructed by Root stood the U.S. Army War College (USAWC). Founded in 1901, this postgraduate military school was intended to prevent another fiasco like the one attending the Army's preparations for the Spanish-American War. Although the Officer Corps had generally performed well at the tactical level in that conflict, senior officers had proven themselves to be "almost completely unprepared to handle the problems of sudden mobilization, training, and the widespread deployment of military forces."[6]

The college was intended to provide advanced study for senior Army officers. Initially, however, it functioned as the War Department's General Staff. USAWC students would, under faculty supervision, work on projects assigned by the War Department. In 1903, Congress approved the formation of a General Staff, precipitating a shift of the staff function away from the USAWC. In the ensuing years, the USAWC gradually morphed into a true military educational institution.[7]

The Army closed the schools at Leavenworth and the USAWC when the United States entered World War I in 1917 and assigned their instructors to positions supporting the war effort. Leavenworth graduates in particular played a noteworthy role in the prosecution of the war in France. A "Leavenworth Clique," in fact, held a near monopoly on the very highest level staff appointments in the American Expeditionary Force (AEF). Nine of the 12 principals on General John Pershing's staff, both of the Army chiefs of staff, and nine out of 10 of the corps' chiefs of staff had attended the staff college. The operational skill and knowledge of these graduates was greatly needed and greatly appreciated. Their worth was particularly evident when their performance was held up against that of nongraduates. Pershing set up a school for staff officers at Langres, France, in the hope of raising the quality of staff work throughout the AEF, which he felt left much to be desired, up to something approaching Leavenworth standards. The performance of staff college graduates in World War I ensured the school of a significant future role in Army education and, as one AEF veteran noted, "put Leavenworth on the map."[8]

The basic system of officer development instituted by Secretary Root remained in place after World War I, albeit enlarged and refined. At the junior officer level, the Army revamped and extended its network of branch schools to keep pace with technological innovations and organizational changes. By the eve of World War II, there were 19 such schools in operation. The Command and General Staff College (CGSC) at Fort Leavenworth, KS, grew in stature and prestige during the interwar years. Attendance at the college, in fact, became a mark of professional distinction and a virtual prerequisite for high rank. An important addition to senior officer professional education during this era came with the creation of the Army Industrial College, Washington, DC, in 1924. This institution was part of a more comprehensive scheme elaborated in the aftermath of World War I to enable the Army to meet more effectively the demands of modern industrialized warfare.[9]

The post-World War I school system concentrated on preparing the Regular Army's (RA) small Officer Corps to lead a vastly expanded citizen Army in the event of a national emergency. Officers had to be ready to lead and manage organizations many times larger than any the War Department could cobble together in peacetime. Accordingly, the orientation of this system, from branch schools all the way up to the war college, tended to be narrowly military.

Even at the USAWC, where military affairs were taught alongside national policy matters, the emphasis was on preparing officers for future command and staff responsibilities rather than on acquainting them with the broader political and economic aspects of national strategy. While these broader considerations were not neglected entirely, of course, they were largely overshadowed by what seemed to be more pressing and immediate priorities.[10]

THE ARMY SCHOOL SYSTEM
IN WORLD WAR II

During World War II, Army schools were again reconfigured, this time to train vast numbers of officers for specific duties and immediate requirements. The educational facets of the school system were drastically cut back or eliminated entirely. General Lesley McNair, head of the Army Ground Forces for most of the war and the officer responsible for training Soldiers for ground combat, wanted to limit formal training along with time spent in the school system as much as possible. He operated under the premise that excessive schooling destroyed initiative and the urge for self-study. In his opinion, practical, on-the-job training in tactical units was the best preparation for leadership in combat. It was a philosophy with many adherents in the Officer Corps, both at the time and subsequently.[11]

THE ARMY SCHOOL SYSTEM IN THE POST-WORLD WAR II ERA

In the war's last stages, the Army began to turn its attention to the post-war configuration of its system for training and educating officers. The War Department wanted to ensure that the lessons of the last war were not forgotten. Prominent among those lessons was the need for a more thorough grasp of joint operations, as well as a better understanding of the strengths and weaknesses of the other services on the part of officers. The Gerow Board met in early-1946 to fashion a plan for the post-war school system. Its recommendations led to, among other things, the establishment of the National War College and the Armed Forces Staff College in Washington, DC, both of which were devoted to the joint training of officers. Three years later, the Department of the Army Board on the Educational System for Army Officers was convened under Lieutenant General Manton S. Eddy to review the adequacy and scope of that system. The

Eddy Board resulted in a more definitive structuring of the officer educational system, the reestablishment of the USAWC, and a more centralized direction of the Army school network.[12]

The message running through the reports of both the aforementioned bodies was that preparation for combat was the central object of the Army's school system. The Army's other roles and missions were considered to be of a decidedly secondary importance. This message was forcefully affirmed by the Eddy Board in its report. "The objective of the Army school system," it declared, "can be stated concisely. It is to prepare an officer to perform effectively those duties to which he may reasonably expect to be assigned in war, with emphasis on the art of command."[13]

This is not to say that senior Army leaders were oblivious to the new dimensions that the Cold War, technological progress, and changing nature of the military profession had brought to military affairs. In fact, they understood that the military profession now had to be viewed in a broader social, economic, and political context than it had in the past and that modern officers needed a wide range of executive and intellectual talents to meet the multifarious and complex demands placed on them. These new development requirements were acknowledged by the Gerow Board, which observed that in the new, post-war world, traits such as initiative, resourcefulness, and the capacity for "constructive thought" were essential for the officer who hoped to keep up with the rapid changes that were transforming the military profession.[14] Still, officer education and training demonstrated more continuity than change. Although the boundaries of the military realm had become more porous, the emphasis of Army schools, along with the officer development system they supported, remained focused on preparation for combat and operational and tactical level assignments.

This emphasis was reaffirmed in 1958 by the Williams Board. Tasked by the Army Chief of Staff to evaluate the "appropriateness" of service school and service college missions, it concluded that the objective of the Army system of officer education and training should remain as prescribed in Army policy and regulations, i.e.:

> to prepare selected individuals of all components of the Army to perform those duties which they may be called upon to perform in war. The emphasis is on the art of command.[15]

Given this focus (as well as what some characterized as the innate conservatism and anti-intellectualism of military leaders), it is not surprising that even the USAWC continued emphasizing the practical, the operational, and the immediately useful over the theoretical, the strategic, and the long term.

Attempts to broaden the USAWC curriculum in the 1950s often encountered stiff resistance. Even minor changes sometimes unleashed a barrage of complaints about how the curriculum was becoming too "academic" and diluted with "theoretical" and historical subjects that contributed little to the development of practical know-how and operational ability in students. Thus, instruction at the USAWC continued on the path that it had been on in the interwar years, with courses demanding only a low level of abreaction and its curriculum resembling training more than education. The result was a school system that, although effective in imparting the mechanics of the military profession, was not particularly adept at cultivating imagination, creativity, and analytical ability in future Army leaders.[16]

THE ARMY SCHOOL SYSTEM IN THE 1960s

With the coming of the John Kennedy administration in 1961, civil-military relations within the government took on a rather troublesome and contentious aspect. President Kennedy, Attorney General Robert Kennedy, and William Fulbright, chief of the powerful Senate Foreign Relations Committee, expressed reservations about the quality of opinion and advice they received from military leaders. The new Secretary of Defense, Robert S. McNamara, made it plain that he did not think that the Officer Corps was, as a body, up to the task of meeting the broad range of requirements necessary to run a complex military organization. As one officer observed, McNamara wanted planners and thinkers but instead got mere warriors.[17]

Thaddeus Holt, Deputy Under Secretary of the Army from 1965 to 1967, also entertained misgivings about intellectual talent among the senior officers he worked with in the Pentagon. "I am not sure," he wrote, "that the collective contribution of the military to the larger policy making process is always up to a high standard." He noted the "inability" of senior Army leaders to "analyze problems systematically and in a broad context and to present alternatives and defend recommendations in an articulate fashion."[18]

Open conflict soon broke out between uniformed leaders and their civilian superiors. Tensions between McNamara's army of young "whiz kids" and senior military officers led to some embarrassing confrontations. It was very difficult for senior officers to have an analyst many years their junior and, with little or no military background, tell them that they did not have an understanding of the military problem at hand. The controversy and in-fighting that arose within the Pentagon led to the early retirement of some senior officers and to constant friction between the executive and congressional branches of government.[19]

Even before the Kennedy/McNamara years, Army leaders had become increasingly aware of the need for a wider and deeper array of intellectual talent within the Officer Corps. In the 1940s and 1950s, the Gerow, Eddy, and Williams Boards had all noted the need for a broader range of talents among officers. A Deputy Chief of Staff for Personnel (DCSPER) study done in the late-1950s also concluded that the Army was not building the expertise necessary to manage effectively its complex and wide-ranging responsibilities. As a result, a growing number of Army leaders had become convinced that the Army did not possess the intellectual capital demanded by its full range of roles and missions that the nation expected. Still, it was the shock administered by McNamara to the Pentagon's entrenched uniformed establishment that finally moved the services to consider fundamental changes in the ways they developed their officers.[20]

There were, of course, profound external forces driving the Army toward a reevaluation of officer development as well. Since 1945, transformations in technology, international affairs, and the ways of warfare made a reevaluation imperative, as did the Army's rapidly expanding responsibilities in the 1960s and early-1970s. In 1965, then Army Chief of Staff Harold K. Johnson announced that the Army was adding "nation-building" to its traditional missions of defending against external threats and ensuring domestic order.

Confronted with insurgencies that threatened the international balance of power, political leaders called upon the military services to help friendly governments in the underdeveloped world quell internal disorder and build a foundation for economic and social progress.

To meet its new mandate, the Army needed officers proficient in foreign languages, conversant with foreign cultures, and capable of performing the many duties and responsibilities encompassed under the rubric of civil affairs. The importance of nation-building as an Army mission was reaffirmed in the late-1960s with the propagation of the Richard Nixon doctrine. That doctrine put a premium on officer education across the entire spectrum of social, economic, political, and military measures that would make for successful U.S. stability and counterinsurgency efforts.[21]

In the mid-1960s, the federal government began pressuring the services to take a more active role in solving some of the nation's "serious domestic problems." Riots, crime, juvenile delinquency, poverty, unemployment, an underperforming educational system, and a host of other societal maladies were, as officials in the Lyndon Johnson and Nixon administrations pointed out, tearing apart the social fabric of the nation and undermining national security. The Army possessed an abundance of leaders with the special skills, abilities, and knowledge necessary to develop and administer social programs that could attack these ills. Many civilian officials saw no logical reason why the Armed Forces should not be used in this way.[22]

As a result of its expanded global and domestic responsibilities, the Army began to revise the curricula in its school system to encompass the wide array of subjects and topics deemed necessary. The intent was to go beyond training officers as highly competent commanders and produce intellectually astute and innovative leaders who were capable of understanding complex issues, be they command-related or not. This new spirit touched all rungs of the Officer Education System (OES), although it was particularly evident at higher levels where the emphasis on the social, political, and technological aspects of national strategy was the strongest.

Two review boards convened during this period provide some insight into the direction officer development was taking: the Haines Board (1966) and the Norris Review (1971). Both made truly transformative recommendations which, while not fully enacted, did more to change the officer developmental process than anything else since the end of World War II. The Haines Board concluded that the Army's school system should shift focus from preparing officers for their next assignment and instead concentrate on the "professional" aspects of a military career.

Such an orientation, appropriate to varying degrees for all rungs of the system, was deemed particularly important at the CGSC and the USAWC. Courses at these institutions, the board asserted, should be geared more toward studies and related to national strategy and international affairs and only secondarily toward "Army problems" and the functioning of higher level staffs. The board quoted approvingly one general officer's thumbnail assessment of the Army's school system, which characterized the existing system of officer education and training as obsolete. It paralleled:

> very closely those which obtained prior to World War II. They [i.e., the schools] have not advanced abreast

of the times . . . there is a tendency to reject insertion into the curriculum of subjects or courses (personnel and business management, politico-military affairs, history, economics) that are not purely military but which are needed to train officers for the wide variety of tasks and assignments they will be called upon to fill.[23]

Another theme of the Haines Board was that schools should place more stress on education and less on training. Instead of drilling students in the "technicalities" of their profession, board members insisted, they should be encouraged to question established practices, experiment with new concepts, and try new practices, procedures, and techniques. Courses should have sufficient depth and substance to provide a meaningful and satisfying intellectual experience to officers, which they currently did not. This would not only improve cognitive capacity and decisionmaking powers but also constitute a powerful retention tool for the intelligent and ambitious.[24]

To give Army courses more rigor and intellectual validity, the board proposed that the school system enter into a closer relationship with the civilian academic community. As things were, Army schools were "inbred" and generally isolated from the "mainstream of academic thought." This was largely true even at the higher levels of the Army school system. School authorities, the board proposed, should reach out to the civilian academic community by attending conferences such as those sponsored by the Association of Higher Education, the Association of American Colleges, and various universities and, at the same time, engage distinguished civilian scholars and educators to review various aspects of the military education system and provide recommendations for improvements.[25]

The conclusions of the Norris Review were, in many respects, similar to that of the Haines Board. The review identified several challenges facing the Army Officer Corps and its school system in the 1970s. The nation's Vietnam driven anti-militarism, educational explosion, and social revolution would all have a significant impact on the way the Army trained its leaders. These developments, the review concluded, posed thorny "socio-psychological" issues that added "a new dimension of difficulty and complexity" to the Army's expanding range of missions.[26] Effective communication with the civilian scientific and technological communities, it noted, called for officers who had a level of education and expertise essentially equivalent to their civilian colleagues. Collectively, the Officer Corps would have to possess a wider and deeper set of talents in an era where technology was exponentially expanding knowledge creation.[27] If the Army did not adjust to these new realities, the review warned, it would find itself being left behind in the race for relevance, societal stature, and funding. It was a view that resonated reasonably well in the Officer Corps during the period under review.[28]

For the officer development process, this meant, according to the Norris Review, that Army schools would have to emphasize education over training and cultivate a closer working relationship with the civilian academic world. In addition, the review argued for equipping officers with a greater understanding of all the external factors that were impinging on and threatening to disrupt the military profession. Thus, instead of imparting factual knowledge and teaching techniques, the Army school system would have to focus on the development of conceptual thinking, critical judgment, and creativity in its officers.[29]

OFFICER GRADUATE EDUCATION, 1946 TO 1973

Another lens through which one can view and assess officer development is the strength of the full-time graduate education program administered by the Army. Officer graduate education dates back to June 1775 when medical officers began attending schools that prepared them to be military physicians. After a period of relative dormancy, the Army's emphasis on graduate work was renewed in 1867, following an assessment of operations during the Civil War. Army doctors, dentists, and veterinarians were the first to benefit from the new policy. Shortly thereafter, however, other officers began receiving advanced training in ballistics, metallurgy, and engineering sciences at civilian institutions. Later, business administration was added to the mix. This civil schooling program gradually expanded until, by the onset of World War I, it had reached a substantial size.[30]

In a legal sense, the beginning of the program can be traced to the National Defense Act of 1916, which allowed for up to 8 percent of the Officer Corps to undertake graduate studies (although nothing near that percentage was ever reached). A damper was placed on the program in the early-1920s by a cost-conscious Congress. The National Defense Act of 1920 stipulated that graduate level education for officers must meet officially recognized and specific Army requirements. This meant the flow of officers into graduate training would be severely curtailed.[31]

In 1927, the U.S. Military Academy (USMA) started sending officers to civilian institutions for graduate work in a few chosen fields such as English and the social sciences. These officers pursued their degrees at night and during the summer when classes were not in session. The Corps of Engineers and some of the technical services also adopted this practice. Later, the Army sent selected officers to China, Japan, France, and Mexico to study languages; to Harvard to study business administration; and to universities such as MIT to study engineering and other "technical" subjects. The numbers involved were not great. A 1938 report recorded that just over 1 percent of the Officer Corps was engaged in graduate study; the percentage of officers actually attaining master's degrees was even smaller. Graduate training, after all, was intended to fill a specific need, not to enhance the academic credentials of the officer.[32]

It was during World War II that the need for greater depth and breadth of officer education became evident. As a result, the Army's graduate education program took off in 1946. Due largely to the efforts of the Gerow Board, the initial post-war batch of 164 officer-students began graduate studies in June 1946.[33]

The Cold War had stimulated an extension of the boundaries of the military profession. Senior officers now, many realized, had to be conversant with diplomacy, foreign trade, and industrial and technological development, along with the political, economic, social, and scientific aspects of national strategy to a much greater degree than in decades past. Accordingly, after 1946, a gradually increasing number of officers were sent to graduate training to master the complexities that now fell into the Army's domain. Between 1946 and 1962, that number rose from 164 to 554.[34]

A coterie of congressional and military leaders provided a steady drum roll of support for advanced civil education for officers in the decade and a half after World War II. The Gerow Board had recommended that the 2 percent cap placed on officers attending graduate programs be removed, maintaining that 5 percent of authorized strength was a more realistic percentage. By 1948, Congress was prepared to exceed that percentage, authorizing the Secretary of the Army to send to up to 8 percent of both RA and reserve component officer strength to graduate school. In 1952, Congress broadened the program to include training with industrial and commercial institutions. Six years later, the Williams Board registered yet another plea for an enlarged civilian schooling program. Not only did the numbers of slots requiring a graduate degree have to be enlarged, the board argued, but slots also had to be filled using a more realistic manning formula. As it was, one officer was allotted to each vacancy. This did not allow officers to complete other career enhancing assignments and left no room for rapid expansion, emergency conditions, or changes in national policy. The board suggested that three of four officers should be trained for each position.[35]

During the Harry Truman and Dwight Eisenhower administrations, these impulses for an enlarged and more robust graduate school program were constrained by fiscal realities, heavy operational demands, and the entrenched view in some quarters that officers should work principally in the operational realm and simply did not need graduate level education. Officers were to be sent to graduate school only to the extent necessary to meet specific, carefully calculated requirements. This policy played well in Congress and with successive administrations, where fiscal discipline was a prime concern. As in the military education system, the emphasis was on immediate payback and short-term savings rather than on long-term value.[36]

After 1960, however, the civil schooling program became progressively more robust. Indeed, the 1960s and the early-1970s were, in many respects, the golden age of fully funded graduate education in the Army. Validated requirements for officers with advanced degrees doubled between 1960 and 1965. Over the subsequent 5 years, these requirements nearly doubled again. Moreover, the Army's officer inventory grew, allowing the ratio of officers studying per validated higher education requirements to rise sharply. The cause of graduate education was helped along by the creation of the Army Educational Requirements Board (AERB) in 1963. By permitting a more precise determination of advanced civil schooling requirements, the AERB paved the way for greater congressional and Department of Defense (DoD) acceptance of stated Army needs.[37]

While technological innovation and increasing global and domestic responsibilities created pressure to expand officer graduate level education, individual prestige and institutional credibility were additional factors pushing the Army in this direction. The Williams Board had observed that a growing number of officers viewed master's degrees as a sign of professional and societal status. The Haines Board made the point with even greater force, arguing that the baccalaureate degree was "no longer the hallmark of an educated man."[38] By the mid-1960s, about 25 percent of college students entered into a graduate program shortly after graduation. At the nation's most selective institutions, this percentage was as high as 90 percent. Indeed, authorities at some of these top end institutions were reluctant to admit students who did not aspire to a doctorate or professional degree. This might seem "somewhat extreme" to the layman, the Williams Board noted, but it reflected the conviction of "academicians in the vanguard of education today." If the military profession wanted to be viewed in the same light as other respected professions, the board insisted, it would have to ensure that its practitioners possessed the requisite educational credentials.[39]

Prestige became an even more salient consideration in the 1960s after Secretary Robert McNamara and his "whiz kids" assumed leadership of the Pentagon. Senior leaders in the Department of the Army, who often had little experience or background in the functional areas they were assigned to superintend, were called upon to evaluate and defend a variety of complicated initiatives. While their broad based military experience had prepared them well for previous command positions, it was frequently not effective in preparing them for what they now had to contend. They often appeared confused and incompetent when confronted by specialists from the DoD, the Bureau of the Budget, or Congress. When dealing with experts, they discovered that intuition and general background knowledge were often inadequate substitutes for true subject matter expertise.[40]

The frequently displayed inability of some of its senior members to deal with complex issues and stand up to expert questioners instilled a sense of intellectual inferiority and professional self-doubt in the Officer Corps. To some, it seemed the military profession was being hijacked by a corps of highly educated civilian elitists who accorded little respect to the intellectual abilities of Soldiers. If Army leaders hoped to reestablish control over the military profession, some concluded, they would have to develop an intellectual ability rivaling that of their civilian counterparts in DoD.[41]

Finally, opportunities for advanced schooling were believed key to retention among junior officers. Rising educational aspirations among younger Americans were making it difficult for the Army to retain talented lieutenants and captains. Studies conducted at the time showed that the higher the education level and the higher the selectivity of undergraduate institution attended, the more likely it was for the officer to leave the service at the earliest opportunity. Both the Haines Board and the Norris Review asserted that graduate education was key to keeping talented officers in the service. If the Army did not expand its fully funded graduate programs, these reviews cautioned, it might find itself "behind the educational power curve" and increasingly unable to compete with civilian industry.[42]

THE ARMY SCHOOL SYSTEM IN THE AGE OF THE ALL-VOLUNTEER FORCE, 1973-85

With the advent of the All-Volunteer Force (AVF) in 1973, the Army's OES finally experienced a transformation. This was driven by, among other things, a redefinition of the threat and a reevaluation of the Army's missions. Many senior leaders had been disheartened by the Vietnam experience and were anxious for the Army to put that conflict behind it. As the war in Southeast Asia wound down, they increasingly turned their attention to the growing threat posed by the Soviet Union and its Warsaw Pact allies in Europe. General William E. DePuy, the first chief of the Training and Doctrine Command (TRADOC), and his deputy, General Paul F. Gorman, took the lead in strategically refocusing the Army to deal with the international realities of the 1970s—realities that were more easily grasped and cleanly defined that those that had confronted the Army during Vietnam.

When Depuy assumed his new duties at Fort Monroe, he had two overriding priorities: rectifying the mistakes he believed the Army made during Vietnam and preparing it for the challenges posed by the Warsaw Pact in Europe. The Soviets had built up a powerful and well-trained army that was thought capable of quickly overwhelming the motley collection of units that the North Atlantic Treaty Organization (NATO) allies could throw up against them. DePuy and Gorman's formula for combating this threat was based in part on the lessons they drew from the Arab-Israeli War of 1973. That conflict demonstrated the greatly increased lethality of weapons that had been developed over the previous decade. It also highlighted the need for better tactical training, well-drilled crews, skilled tactical commanders, and combined arms coordination. These lessons shaped the U.S. Army's vision of modern war. TRADOC soon became absorbed in distilling new, clear doctrinal prescriptions derived from that vision and focused specifically on conditions in Central Europe.

To that end, DePuy implemented what he called a "back to basics" approach to officer development. Concerned that training in the Army had "almost disappeared," he pushed the Army school system away from what he considered undue emphasis upon higher education and back toward tactical training. Accordingly, officer schools, from the pre-commissioning level all the way up to the USAWC, were told to concentrate on preparing officers for their next assignment. The Army must be prepared, DePuy and

Gorman emphasized, to win the first battle of the next war. Long-term professional development and the building of critical thinking skills, which the Haines Board wanted to promote, were to be put on the back burner. Military proficiency and "tactical competence" were now the Army's watchwords.

Generals DePuy and Gorman agreed that what was needed was a "train-evaluate-train" methodology that held Soldiers of all ranks to strict performance standards. This methodology was embedded in DePuy's famous "systems approach to training" (SAT). The SAT consisted of five interrelated phases: analysis, design, development, implementation, and evaluation. All training in the Army was reconfigured gradually to adhere to this SAT model.[43]

This emphasis upon tactical proficiency and technical competence did not abate upon DePuy's retirement but continued with undiminished ardor over the next decade. In the spring of 1977, an "agreement" was reached among senior leaders about the existing (and unsatisfactory) state of officer training and education in the Army. Due primarily to a lack of funds, that agreement contended that the Army's school system was still not producing officers with "the desired level of military competency" envisaged by DePuy and Gorman. Shortly thereafter, Chief of Staff General Bernard Rogers directed Major General B. L. Harrison to conduct a thorough review of the way that the Army educated and trained its officers. The result was the landmark *Review of Education and Training for Officers* (RETO), a study that set the direction for the school system and the officer development process for the rest of the Cold War and beyond.[44]

The RETO report stressed the importance of officers mastering the knowledge and skills "unique to the military profession." The principal purpose of the school system, it insisted, was to prepare officers for "war fighting." In the basic and advanced courses, lieutenants and captains should acquire the skills necessary to operate small units. At the CGSC and the USAWC, field grade officers should acquire the skills necessary to lead larger units.[45]

Contrasting the RETO recommendations for the USAWC curriculum with those of the earlier Haines Board brings their differences into stark relief. As noted earlier, the Haines Board concluded that the military profession was being increasingly affected by a variety of social, political, economic, and scientific factors. Consequently, an Officer Corps that understood only purely "Army" matters was insufficient. Those officers designated for high level assignments needed to be familiar with subjects, disciplines and perspectives that transcended the military art — subjects, disciplines, and perspectives that would permit them to understand and intelligently shape national strategy and foreign policy.

The RETO report fundamentally differed from this view, emphasizing training over education and recommending a shift of the USAWC curriculum back toward the military arts. The USAWC, it asserted, should be focused on the command and control of large units (corps level and above). More instruction should be given in joint and combined operations in a "coalition warfare environment" and more attention devoted to such topics as emergency action procedures, force planning and structuring, and the "strategic deployment and tactical employment of large units marshaled on short notice for specific purposes." Courses on foreign policy, history, economics, political science, and other subjects that did not directly relate to ground combat did not play a large role in the USAWC RETO scheme.[46]

The next major review of officer professional development was the *Professional Officer Development Study* (PDOS) published in 1985. Like the Haines Board and the RETO study, the PDOS reflected the direction the Army's school system was going. Its basic themes were similar to those presented by the RETO group. The PDOS was written at a time when the Army was under attack by observers within and outside the military who charged that the Officer Corps was not prepared "for war and combat" and that the officer development process was too focused upon producing efficient peacetime managers rather than effective combat leaders.[47]

The PDOS largely acknowledged the validity of these charges.[48] Its authors asserted that the principal mission of the Army's educational system was to prepare leaders to win on the battlefield. As things stood, they noted, there was a lack of focus on "war fighting and combat action" in officer education and training. The study recommended that Army schools reorient instruction to produce "technically and tactically proficient" officers capable of effectively employing weapons systems, prepared for their next assignment, and, perhaps above all, possessing the "warrior spirit." Technical competence, tactical skill, and the ability to appropriately apply doctrine were essential components of this spirit. Whenever possible, the necessary skills and competencies were to be acquired through "hands-on field training," which was considered to be the most effective method of learning. Moreover, the PDOS underscored the importance of time spent in troop units, which was not only the best preparation for their wartime duties but was vital to unit readiness and the overall state of training in the Army. Thus, the Army officer development system of the late-1980s accelerated the emphasis on training begun under DePuy and Gorman in 1973.[49]

GRADUATE EDUCATION IN THE AGE OF THE ALL-VOLUNTEER FORCE

Given the previous discussion, it is not surprising that the Army's commitment to, and emphasis upon, fully funded graduate education for officers gradually eroded after 1973. That erosion was reflected in the sharp drop in validated positions for graduate degree holders in the officer inventory. By this measure, the apogee of graduate education in the Army took place in 1972. Thereafter, the trend was downward. Between the end of the Vietnam war and the Grenada intervention, the number of officer positions certified by the AERB as needing a graduate degree fell by about 37 percent. This decline, it is important to note, was steeper and more rapid than the overall reduction in officer strength that took place in this period (it declined by about 23 percent).

Certainly, the high cost of fully funded graduate education was a powerful force behind this downward trend. Calls for a scaling back of the program began to grow in frequency and intensity as the services withdrew from Southeast Asia and as pressures on the defense budget mounted. In 1973, the Government Accountability Office (GAO) published a report that was highly critical of advanced degree programs in the services—at least those that took officers out of units for extended periods of time. That report found a host of management irregularities in the program. First, the criteria that the services used to identify positions requiring graduate work, the GAO reported, were "so broad and permissive" that they were practically worthless. Not only were these criteria excessively broad, but they were also inconsistently applied. In their survey of 14 military installations, GAO researchers found many "validated" positions where the need for a graduate degree was questionable at best. At continental U.S. (CONUS) Army headquarters, for example, five assistant chaplain positions were certified as needing graduate degrees in comptrollership. Moreover, most officers who had been sent to earn an advanced degree were not working in their designated specialty. Almost 70 percent of the officers surveyed were found to be in this category. The picture that the GAO painted was of a program out of control.[50]

The GAO urged that the fully funded graduate education should be approved only when it was an "essential prerequisite" for the satisfactory performance of duty. In addition, it suggested that less expensive alternatives such as appropriate work experience, short training courses, and partially funded, "after hours" graduate programs be substituted for full-time study. The civilianization of validated positions was another alternative it championed.[51]

The DoD challenged the report, contending that the GAO failed to recognize the "intangible" value and benefits of graduate education. Of particular concern to the DoD was the GAO's failure to acknowledge: a) the rising educational aspirations of the segment of the population from which the services had to recruit military officers; b) the value of graduate education to ongoing junior officer retention efforts; and c) the increased capability that an officer with graduate level education brought to billets that lay outside the scope of his or her academic credentials. Graduate study, the DoD noted in regard to the last point, contributes to the intellectual development of officers, cultivating the capacity for "original thought" and promoting "the development of analytical tools for problem solving."[52]

The authors of the GAO report were unimpressed by DoD's rebuttal. They countered that the supposed benefits of graduate education must be weighed against its substantial costs and the extended periods that officers participating in the program were away from their normal duties. In their report to Congress, they recommended that more "stringent criteria" should be applied to the validation of graduate positions and that full-time graduate education should be kept within strict limits. The utilitarian approach to advanced study espoused by the GAO would steadily gain traction over the next decade.[53]

In subsequent years, reports by other federal agencies exposed similar shortcomings in and came to similar conclusions about fully funded graduate education in the services. During the same period, Congress and the DoD subjected the budgets for graduate education to closer and closer scrutiny. The effects of these developments were cumulative—graduate level educational opportunities for officers steadily eroded away.

Insight into just how far graduate study had fallen in the Army's post-Vietnam officer developmental system can be gained by juxtaposing the Haines Board and the Norris Review, on the one hand, with the RETO report and the PDOS, on the other. The former underlined the importance of fashioning an Officer Corps possessed of broad vision, critical thinking skills, and the wide range of academic and intellectual talents needed to run a modern military establishment. The emphasis was clearly on education, as opposed to training, and on close cooperation with the civilian academic community. Graduate schooling was a high priority. Indeed, there was a fear that if the Army did not raise the collective intellectual acumen of its officers, the military profession itself might be taken over by civilian interlopers.

The RETO report and the PDOS differed markedly. Both can be seen as a reaction by those leaders who thought the Army of the 1960s and early-1970s went too far in accommodating the values and norms of the civilian world. In these documents, military proficiency, technical competence, and tactical skill were the overarching themes. What the Army needed, the PDOS and RETO report implied, was not scholars but warriors, not managers but leaders, not military executives but commanders and, in the Army School System, not education but training. The skills and proficiencies necessary to meet mission requirements and reassert uniformed leadership over the military profession were not to be developed through intellectual exercises in classrooms but through rigorous "hands-on training" in a field environment and service in tactical units.

Thus, in the environment in which the Army found itself after Vietnam, graduate school lost much of its luster. At a West Point Founder's Day celebration in 1976, one distinguished retired four-star general — one known for his wide learning and intellectual prowess — roundly denounced the Advanced Civil Schooling (ACS) program. He asserted that officers should not be pursuing graduate degrees in academic disciplines, which he clearly regarded as frivolous for the professional Soldier. Instead, in his opinion, they should be focused on earning a master's degree "in the Army," by which he meant getting as much experience as possible in career-enhancing tactical assignments. His remarks were greeted with enthusiastic applause.[54]

Some have interpreted the decline of the Army's officer graduate degree program after 1973 as a sign of the institution's long-standing and deeply rooted anti-intellectualism. There had always been present within the Officer Corps, to paraphrase Thaddeus Holt, a disdain for those whose work entails not the accomplishment of tangible and immediately evident results but passive observation and analysis. With the advent of the AVF, this anti-intellectualism seemed to gain strength steadily as the Army's strategic focus shifted as the memories of Vietnam faded, and as the institutional self-doubt of the 1960s and early-1970s gave way to a robust confidence. Many officers began to feel that perhaps the civilian academic community had as much to learn from them as they did from the civilian academic community.

CONCLUSION

Since World War II, the evolution of officer education and training (and to an extent the officer development process itself) has been shaped by a number of factors, both internal and external to the Army. Externally controlled factors included strategic priorities, the Army's roles and missions, political and social pressures, and, of course, budgetary realities, while internally controlled factors entailed operational needs and doctrine and personnel policies (especially officer recruiting and retention).

In absolute terms, the decade and a half after World War II was a period in which training and tactical experience trumped professional and graduate education in the world of officer professional development. In the Army school system, the focus, from pre-commissioning through the USAWC, was on preparation for command and the next assignment. While it is true that, in recognition of technological advances and the complexities of the new strategic situation brought on by the Cold War, graduate education experienced a steady, if gradual, expansion; it was held within strict bounds and limited to specific purposes. Fiscal austerity explains some of this but so, too, does the prevailing view that graduate school was peripheral to the military profession, good perhaps for a small body of experts but not an avenue taken by officers on the road to high rank and professional distinction.

The 1960s and the early-1970s witnessed a noticeable shift in the Army's priorities and orientation. In the Army school system, this was manifested by a renewed stress on professional education and a concomitant de-emphasis of training. Schools were instructed to make their courses more intellectually challenging, add depth and substance to their curricula, focus on long-term professional development instead of the next assignment, encourage a spirit on inquiry and experimentation, and reach out to civilian educational institutions and associations to enrich the content of their programs. At the same time, the Army's commitment to graduate school deepened. The number of validated positions grew by a factor of four between 1960 and 1970 and almost five by 1972. Moreover, graduate school was no longer perceived to be just for specialists who had given up on promotion to the top ranks of Army leaders. Highly competitive officers now pursued master's degrees and doctoral degrees to bolster their professional resume.

The new view of officer professional development reflected an expanded set of roles and missions, a heightened awareness of the growing complexity of the military profession, a mounting sense of institutional self-doubt induced by the trauma inflicted by a McNamara-dominated defense establishment, societal changes, and a desire to solve the critical junior officer retention problem.

After Vietnam, the Army returned to an earlier conception of the officer development process. The primacy of training and preparation for the next assignment gradually reasserted itself, while professional education and long-term development took a back seat. Unlike the Haines Board (which urged that the school system produce innovative, inquisitive officers with critical thinking skills), the RETO report and the PDOS pushed for technically competent and tactically skilled officers thoroughly imbued with the warrior ethos. Meanwhile, the cause of full-time graduate education suffered a setback. A master's degree from a reputable institution no longer had the professional cachet it did in the 1960s and early-1970s, when even the Army's best and brightest "warriors" vied for a chance to attend graduate school. New strategic priorities and operational doctrines explain some of this, as do budget constraints, public and internal criticism born of operational mishaps such as the ones that occurred in Iran and Grenada, and, as Vietnam receded into the past, a growing sense of institutional self-confidence.

In the four decades after 1945, architects of the Army's officer development process struggled to find the appropriate balance between education and training, between preparation for the immediate and preparation for the long-term, between leadership and management, and between technical competence and intellectual agility. Today, the Army's officer development system operates in essential agreement with the vision articulated by General Depuy in 1973, one that subordinates intellectual and strategic astuteness to tactical and operational expertise. How appropriate it is for an Army trying to make its way in the conceptual age is currently a matter of intense debate.

ENDNOTES - CHAPTER 5

1. Edwin J. Arnold, Jr., *Professional Military Education: Its Historical Development and Future Challenges*, Carlisle, PA: U.S. Army War College, April, 1993, p. 17.

2. William H. Carter, "Post-Graduate Instruction in the United States Army," *Educational Review*, December 1902, p. 435.

3. The School of Application for Cavalry and Field Artillery was established at Fort Riley, KS, in 1904, while a new Artillery School of Fire was created in 1911. A School of Musketry and School of Application were added to the Infantry School in 1907 and 1913, respectively.

4. Carter, p. 436.

5. Almost all the branches were represented in Leavenworth's study body.

6. John W. Masland and Laurence I. Radway, *Soldiers and Scholars: Military Education and National Policy*, Princeton, NJ: Princeton University Press, 1957, pp. 84-86.

7. Otto L. Nelson, *National Security and the General Staff*, Washington, DC: Infantry Journal Press, 1946, p. 70.

8. Timothy K. Nenninger, *The Leavenworth Schools and the Old Army; Education, Professionalism, and the Officer Corps of the United States Army, 1881-1918*, Westport, CT; Greenwood Press, 1978, p. 4; Peter J. Schifferle, *America's School for War: Fort Leavenworth, Officer Education, and Victory in World War II*, Lawrence, KS: Univer-

sity of Kansas Press, 2010, p. 6; Edward M. Coffman, "The American Military Generation Gap in World War I: The Leavenworth Clique in the AEF," William Geffen, *Command and Commanders in Modern Warfare*, Washington, DC: Government Printing Office (GPO), 1968, p. 37.

9. Schifferle, pp. 87-90.

10. *Ibid.*, pp. 96-97.

11. Robert R. Palmer, Bell I. Wiley, and William R. Keast, *The Procurement and Training of Ground Combat Troops*, Washington, DC: Historical Division, Department of the Army, 1948, p. 45.

12. War Department, *Report of the War Department Military Education Board on the Educational System for Officers of the Army*, Washington, DC: Gerow Board, February 17, 1946; pp. 10-11 (hereafter referred to as the Gerow Board Report); Department of the Army, *Report of the Department of the Army Board on Educational System for Officers*, Washington, DC: Eddy Board, June 15, 1949, pp. 7-9 (hereafter referred to as the Eddy Board Report).

13. Eddy Board Report, p. 1.

14. Gerow Board Report, p. 5.

15. Department of the Army, *Report of the Department of the Army Officer Education and Training Review Board*, Washington, DC: Williams Board, 1958, pp. 1, 10 (hereafter referred to as the Williams Board Report).

16. Masland and Radway, pp. 507-509.

17. Allen W. Wiegand, *Military Participation in Systems Analysis*, Carlisle, PA: U.S. Army War College, April, 1966, p. 21.

18. Samuel P. Huntington, "Power, Expertise, and the Military Profession," *Daedalus*, Fall 1963, p. 785; Thaddeus Holt, *The Army Officer Corps and the Pentagon in 1965-1967: Miscellaneous Observations*, Thaddeus Holt, Papers. 1 Box. Carlisle, PA: Archives of the U.S. Army Heritage and Education Center, p. 7.

19. Robert N. Ginsburgh, "The Challenge to Military Professionalism," *Foreign Affairs*, January 1964, pp. 255-268; Cole, pp. iv, 5, 40.

20. Robert J. Baer, *Are We Trimming the Fat or Wasting Needed Talent?* Carlisle, PA: U.S. Army War College, April, 1967, p. 11.

21. Harold K. Johnson, "The Army's Role in Nation Building and Preserving Stability," *Army Information Digest*, November, 1965, pp. 6-13.

22. Robert E. Ayers, *Army Talent in the Domestic Arena*, Carlisle, PA: U.S. Army War College, March 1970, p. 2; Melvin R. Laird, U.S. Secretary of Defense, Memorandum, For Secretaries of the Military Departments, Subject: Domestic Action Council, April 28, 1969.

23. Department of the Army, *Report of the Department of the Army Board to Review Army Officer Schools*, Washington, DC: Haines Board, February 1966, pp. I:27, III:449 (hereafter referred to as the Haines Board Report).

24. *Ibid.*, pp. I:32, III:414.

25. *Ibid.*, p. III:751.

26. Frank W. Norris, *Review of Army Officer Educational System*, Washington, DC: Norris Review, December 1, 1971, pp. 2-1 to pp. 2-10 (hereafter referred to as the Norris Review).

27. *Ibid.*

28. Williams Board Report, p. 223; Norris Review, pp. I:2/5 and 2/6.

29. *Ibid.*, pp. 2-5.

30. Haines Board Report, p. II:263.

31. *Ibid.*, p. II:266.

32. Masland and Radway, p. 88. In 1933, Congress authorized the USMA to award a B.S. degree to its graduates; in part, this authorization was sought to facilitate the enrollment of increasing numbers of regular officers in civilian universities for graduate study, particularly the sciences.

33. *Ibid.*

34. *Ibid.*, pp. 20-21.

35. Gerow Board Report, pp. 7-8; Williams Board Report, p. 35.

36. Haines Board Report, p. II:263; Masland and Radway, p. 508.

37. Haines Board Report, pp. I:17, III:415; Norris Review, p. I:41.

38. Haines Board Report, p. III:457.

39. Williams Board Report, p. 231; Haines Board Report, pp. III:695-696.

40. Minot B. Dodson, *US Regular Army Officers and Graduate Degrees*, Carlisle, PA: U.S. Army War College, May 1963, pp. 24-25.

41. Ginsburgh, p. 258.

42. Haines Board Report, pp. III:415-416; Norris, p. I:8/8.

43. *Review of Education and Training for Officers (RETO)*, Washington, DC: Department of the Army, June 30, 1978, p. I:v (hereafter referred to as the RETO Report).

44. RETO Report, p. I:vi.

45. *Ibid.*, pp. III:2, 8, 15.

46. *Ibid.*, p. III:15.

47. *Professional Development of Officers Study (PDOS)*, Washington, DC: Department of the Army, February 1985, p. I:21 (hereafter referred to as the PDOS); Donald R. Baucom, "The Professional Soldier and the Warrior Spirit," *Strategic Review*, Fall 1985, p. 43; James J. McCleskey III, *The U.S. Army Professional Development of Officers Study: A Critique*, Carlise, PA: U.S. Army War College, March 1986, p. 18.

48. PDOS, p. I:26.

49. *Ibid.*, p. I:34.

50. *Improvements Needed in Determining Graduate Education Requirements for Military Officer Positions*, Report No. B-165558, Washington, DC: GAO, August 28, 1973, pp. 2-3, 15, 22.

51. *Ibid.*, p. 22.

52. *Ibid.*, p. 18.

53. *Ibid.*, p. 20.

54. Personal recollection of the author, who attended this event.

CHAPTER 6

EMPLOYING OFFICER TALENT

INTRODUCTION

Despite the revolutionary changes that have transformed warfare and the military profession over the last century, the fundamental principles that have guided the employment of officers have survived largely intact. Based on Elihu Root's interpretation of the Prussian military paradigm and the "company man" model used to develop business executives during the industrial age, these principles have taken on the aspect of hallowed tradition. That is not to say, of course, that the Army has been blind to the need for change. Concessions, and in some cases significant concessions, have been made to specialization and "functionalization," developments that run directly counter to the "company man" paradigm. Nevertheless, the broad outlines of the officer employment patterns laid out at the beginning of the 20th century, albeit modified and refined, are still clearly recognizable today.

This chapter will sketch with very broad strokes the policies and the underlying philosophical and operational assumptions that have guided the employment of officers since the end of World War I. In the process, it will outline the story of how personnel managers have struggled, with only limited success, to place the right officer in the right position and still satisfy the demands of the traditional career progression model. As in previous chapters, this one will begin in the interwar years and end in the 1980s, when the Office of Economic and Manpower Analysis (OEMA) "employing officer talent" monograph essentially picks up the story.

INTERWAR YEARS

Shortly after the conclusion of World War I, the Army articulated a career progression model that it used, to the extent that it could given the strictures under which it operated, to shape an Officer Corps capable of leading a vastly expanded citizen Army in the event of a national emergency. This model served as the theoretical foundation upon which officer assignments were made.

The ideal career pattern under this system entailed rotation through a variety of assignments at progressively higher levels. By following this path, the officer, it was expected, would become familiar with the full range of duties and responsibilities needed to command at high levels. One interwar U.S. Army War College (USAWC) student provided a succinct summary of the philosophy behind officer assignments:

> An officer must be thoroughly acquainted with the various activities of the Army of the United States and that this requires a variety of duties giving him first a practical knowledge of his branch, second, the regular army, and third, the other components of the Army. To have this varied experience a limit of four years on a specific duty has been generally practiced. In general, the officer should not repeat any job.[1]

Troop duty was the cornerstone of this model. Service in tactical units, it was assumed, provided officers with leadership experiences, knowledge, skills, and insights into the psychology of the individual Soldier that simply could not be gained elsewhere. If duty with troops was the cornerstone of this model, preparation for command was its ultimate purpose. This was especially true for combat arms officers, upon whom the burden of command would fall in any future conflict. In addition to command slots, positions on battalion, regimental, and brigade staffs were seen as key assignments because they gave the officer many of the same insights, experiences, and knowledge that service as a commander did. Duty with the Army staff and with the civilian components, although considered important and broadening experiences, were usually reserved for field grade officers who already had mastered the fundamentals of their branch and profession. It was a career pattern that, as historian Richard Yarger suggests, the modern officer could easily relate.[2]

Actual assignments, although based generally on the career progression model just described, were constrained by officer availability, budgets, legislative restrictions (no officer, for example, could spend more than 4 years in Washington, DC, on the General Staff), the need to garrison overseas posts, and various policy restrictions. Of those policy restrictions, fairness or "equity of duty" was one of the most salient for personnel managers, who wanted to distribute both the pleasure and the pain of service more or less uniformly across the Officer Corps. "Equity of duty" had two important geographic dimensions. First, it meant that officers were to spend roughly the same amount of time on foreign service as their contemporaries of the same grade and branch. Too much foreign service was seen as a hardship and injurious to the family life of an officer. Second, every officer was to receive his fair share of assignments at "good stations" within the United States. In practical terms, this meant that no officer was to receive repeated assignments on either the west or east coasts, where, by general consensus, the duty was the most pleasant. Everyone had to take their turn at posts on the borders and in the Midwest, areas that could not compete with the coasts in terms of quality of life. The concept of fairness as an assignment tenet also extended to units. Every unit or organization was supposed to receive its fair share of high quality officers, as measured by such gauges as officer efficiency reports and general reputation, as well as its share of more marginal performers.[3]

To be sure, there was a general recognition among Army leaders that certain positions required special talents, as the Great War had made painfully obvious. Personnel managers generally strove to fill those positions with officers with the desired talents. The problem was that with the various other considerations that had to be taken into account, it was often difficult to make this match.

POST-WORLD WAR II ERA

The advent of the Cold War moved the Army to reconsider the way it employed its officers. Before World War II, requirements for specialized or particular talents, while present, were not acutely felt. In an emergency, the Army could, as it had in both World War I and World War II, call upon civilian specialists and experts to accomplish related military tasks. Friendly nations to the North and South, the ocean barriers, and the nature of war during this period gave strength to this officer employment construct. After 1945, however, uniformed leaders quickly recognized the increasing demand for officers with deep talents in a number of fields. The Army now needed diplomats, statesmen, scientists, economists, and mathematicians, as well as combat leaders.[4]

To accommodate these new demands, in 1948, the Army G-1 published a new guide for career planning. In this guide, the Army announced its intention to employ officers where "their abilities and aptitudes could best be used to accomplish the Army's assigned missions," that is to say, to place the right officer in the right position. At the same time, the Army began to revise its career model to develop officers with deep talents to address a proliferating array of specialized needs. By the mid-1950s, specialist career patterns had been developed for Civil Affairs/Military Government, Army Aviation, Atomic Energy, Research and Development, the Foreign Area Officer (FAO) program, and the Army Security Agency. A number of informal career fields, such as Comptroller, also received *de facto* recognition.[5]

Despite the talk about placing the right officer in the right position and making an accommodation with the specialized personnel demands of the new age, personnel managers, for the most part, continued to steer officers along well-worn career paths. Branch "qualification," the planned and progressive rotation of assignments, and the avoidance of extended or repetitive tours of duty in any one area remained the cornerstones of career development. The Army's guidance to those seeking to develop or employ deep talents was rather confusing (some considered it disingenuous). One Army publication had this to say:

> A specialist who has maintained qualification in his branch need not be apprehensive about his opportunities for promotion . . . provided his overall record compares favorably with that of his non-specialist contemporary.[6]

DA Pamphlet 600-3, Career Planning for Army Officers, noted that:

> The military specialist of greatest value to the Army is primarily qualified in his basic branch and secondarily qualified in one of the specialist career fields. The officer . . . failing to remain qualified in his basic branch is usually of limited potential as a future senior army commander.[7]

With such pronouncements, Army leaders seemed to be talking out of both sides of their mouths. *The Armed Forces Officer* was more straightforward in its guidance to officers:

> . . . those who get to the top have to be many sided men, with skill in the control and guidance of a multifarious variety of activities. Therefore, even the young specialist, who has his eyes on a narrow track because his talents seem to lie in that direction, is well advised to raise his sights and extend his interests to the far horizons of the profession.[8]

The Army, it seems, recognized the new realities of the post-war world but declined to take any really substantive steps to accommodate them. The career progression model predicated on the mass mobilization of a citizen Army had become so deeply ingrained in the consciousness of professional officers that any steps taken to substantially alter traditional officer assignment patterns were certain to be met with stiff resistance.

One of the basic assumptions underlying the employment of officers was that a well-rounded officer was, or at least should be, capable of handling almost any job reasonably well. In fact, what had become military custom by the 1950s dictated that a truly "good man" should be adept at every job regardless of his background or the demands of the position. Accordingly, the Army G-1 assigned officers based on their Military Occupational Specialty (MOS) and their score on the Officer Evaluation Report (OER) efficiency index, essentially an order of merit list for officers within each year group. Demonstrated potential, as evidenced by past performance, was considered far more important than actual experience or specialized training in the employment of officers.[9]

Commanders in the field who were responsible for the execution of certain specialized tasks or functions, however, often rejected the logic of the G-1 and demanded trained or experienced experts to fill particular positions. They did not buy into the assumption that every officer could do every job even at an acceptable level. Experience told them otherwise. Indeed, the frequency and intensity with which commanders bombarded the Pentagon with requests for specific talents greatly irritated and frustrated personnel managers.[10]

Acceptance of the idea that all officers were qualified to perform most assignments (commensurate with their grade and branch) made the life of personnel managers much easier and the officer assignment process run much more smoothly. Officers could obviously be plugged into slots much more easily when this concept prevailed. On the other hand, this conceptual construct did not provide for operational effectiveness. It resulted in officers being assigned "willy-nilly" to personnel, intelligence, and comptroller duties—duties for which many of them were completely unprepared.[11]

Inherent in the career progression model was what one officer labeled a "paradox." The logic of the model demanded that commanders give their subordinates the opportunity to serve in a number of disparate positions to broaden their professional horizons and ensure that they would remain competitive for promotion. To meet the demands of the model, commanders had to sacrifice unit effectiveness, which some refused to do willingly. This tradeoff and its consequences were acknowledged explicitly and sanctioned by the 1948 Army planning guide referred to earlier, which expressed a determination to place the right officer in the right slot. That guide, in fact, manifested a "near complete disregard" for the impact of assignment rotation on the units or organizations affected. "We must destroy the idea," wrote the authors of the guide, "that the principal goal of any peacetime command is unit efficiency."[12]

As in the interwar period, officer assignments were subject to various restrictions and constraints. Availability was one restriction. Even if personnel managers found the right match between an officer and a position, there was no guarantee that the officer would be available for reassignment. Another constraint was "equality of treatment." This principle essentially stated that officers were to be treated equally, serve the same number of years in grade for each rank, and experience roughly the same career pattern. Assignments were thus made within this framework of uniform treatment for all, assuring, it was expected, equal opportunity of promotion through the ranks. This commitment to uniform treatment compromised the development of officers with deep talents since it effectively curtailed the career of anyone who served repetitive tours in a particular field.[13]

The "equitability" of assignments was still another restraint. For example, all officers were to serve their fair share of foreign tours and approximately the same number of short and long tours. Moreover, they were to experience roughly equal amounts of family separation. These considerations made it much more difficult for personnel managers to match talent with needs.

Some insight into the Army's ideas about officer employment can be gained by studying its reaction to the legislation for "responsibility pay" that was passed by Congress in the late-1950s. This type of pay was meant to reward and incentivize officers who were serving in positions involving "unusual responsibility." In the other services, many of the slots so designated were filled by officers with special talents.[14]

The Army rejected the idea of responsibility pay (the legislation authorizing it was permissive in nature) on three grounds. First, it would inhibit the development of an Officer Corps with broad backgrounds capable of handling a wide range of assignments. Many senior officers felt that specialization and leadership could not co-exist within the same individual. Second, it would necessitate additional controls on officer assignments, thus adding to the administrative problems that already plagued officer management. Third, it would not be "fair." Responsibility pay would, as one officer noted, ". . . benefit a few and downgrade many." Indeed, it might even result in the horrifying prospect of a captain earning more than a major.[15]

On the institutional level, the distribution of quality across the Army placed another stricture on officer employment. The rule was to distribute officer quality in such a way so as to ensure that all agencies and units would have a representative slice of officer talent. Ideally, each organization would receive approximately equal shares of the higher quality, middle quality, and lower quality officers—quality being defined as "demonstrated potential" as reflected in officer efficiency reports. This uniform distribution of "talent" was never achieved, but it was a factor in the assignment of officers.[16]

THE 1960s AND EARLY-1970s

The 1960s and early-1970 were crisis years for officer employment. The dramatic technological advances since 1945, the growing complexity of the military profession, the proliferation of service missions and responsibilities, and, with the advent of Robert McNamara as the Secretary of Defense, an increased demand for expert knowledge and specialized experience among senior officers suggested that a new officer employment paradigm was imperative—a paradigm that would place the right officer with the right talents in the right assignment. No longer, said some, could the Army afford to operate on the premise that effectiveness and expertise must take a back seat to the more or less planned incompetence inherent in the traditional officer development model. The Army's sense of crisis during this period was heightened by an officer attrition problem, which ravaged the ranks of lieutenants, captains, and senior field grade officers. This problem resulted in the exodus of the most intellectually talented officers out of the Army, a shortage of officers in several critical fields, and the leakage of talent that the Army desperately needed to address its expanded range of responsibilities. According to many observers, this attrition problem could have been ameliorated by assignment practices that placed more emphasis on aligning skills, education, and experience with positions. [17]

Despite the recognition that the Army needed to revise the way it approached officer assignments, little was done in the way of adaptation. The traditional career path toward developing generalists remained very much alive. Past performance and the imperative to avoid repetitive assignments continued to regulate the employment of officers.

This reliance on the supposedly tried and true manner of developing and employing officers prevented the Army from adequately addressing many of the complex tasks that it was increasingly being asked to shoulder. There were, one USAWC student noted, ". . . seemingly conflicting requirements" for senior military specialists. On the one hand, the Army sought officers adept at managing complex problems arising from technological advancements and the demands of international military statesmanship, yet on the other, it desired "heroic leaders" trained to function effectively as cogs in the Army's vast mobilization machine. One of the shortcomings of the extant system, this officer continued, was that it did not ensure that the full range of officer skills necessary to run a modern defense enterprise were on hand.[18]

The Officer Corps was particularly deficient, some observers noted, in those skills necessary to accomplish the myriad of nonoperational tasks and functions that had fallen under the Army's purview. This was a matter of some concern because since World War II, the number of officers occupied with nonoperational tasks had grown substantially while the percentage employed in branch material duties or assigned to troop units had declined. By the 1960s, for example, only one-third of lieutenant colonels could expect to command a battalion of any kind.[19]

The dearth of nonoperational talent was particularly evident in the Pentagon, where officers were regularly called upon to work and interact with members of Congress, the administration, and various federal agencies on a wide variety of complicated issues. Nevertheless, assignments to the Pentagon, like officer assignments throughout the Army, were based on the general background of the officer concerned and on his score on the OER efficiency index. Often, little or no consideration was given to the specialized nature of the duties and responsibilities involved.[20]

Under Secretary of the Army Thaddeus Holt commented on the bewilderment and frustration that many general officers felt when working at the Department of the Army. Accustomed to having their opinions and decisions uncritically accepted by subordinates and sympathetically considered by their military superiors, they were shocked when their judgments or pronouncements were questioned by high-ranking civilian officials. These generals could not fathom how the thoroughly evaluated products generated by their individual staffs could fail to stand up to the scrutiny of highly educated but militarily inexperienced civilians. After all, the senior members of their staff, like they themselves, had navigated successfully through the military career system and had demonstrated potential for high-level responsibility. The fact that they were now operating in a world where specialized knowledge and a mastery of abstract theory counted for more than a broad background appropriate for overseeing large operational formations apparently did not fully register on them.[21]

One officer discussed the challenges faced by senior military officers in the Office of the Deputy Chief of Staff for Personnel (DCSPER) in the early-1960s. He told of the situation he encountered when he was assigned to that office. "Of the 20-odd division chiefs in the office of the DCSPER," he wrote:

> only five or six had prior experience in personnel work. Yet, these officers occupied positions where they were required to review and defend a wide variety of complicated personnel directives and legislation. While of outstanding general background and intelligence, they were no match for the expert questioners in the Department of Defense, Bureau of the Budget and Congress. This is where the Army loses its shirt. In short, when one is faced with an expert, intuition and general background are not substitutes for knowledge.[22]

The Army's ability to match qualifications with positions was inhibited by a number of factors. One was that the Army remained wedded to the career progression model that focused on molding "a highly competent Officer Corps to serve in positions of progressively higher responsibility." Another impediment was the branch organizational structure. The most qualified officer for a particular position might be found in a career branch other than the one that received the requisition. Nevertheless, there was no simple way of determining that because of the constraints imposed by branch compartmentalization. Thus, organizational stovepipes greatly reduced both assignment flexibility and talent visibility.[23]

The Army's unwavering commitment to fairness in assignments remained a major obstacle to matching qualifications with positions. This was especially evident in the employment of officers identified for service in Military Assistance Advisory Groups (MAAGs). Out of a sense of assignment equity, the Army, as it had done for decades, did not assign officers to repetitive hardship tours. No officer was to "suffer" more than another. Moreover, by retaining this commitment to fairness, the Army hoped to prevent advisors from "going native," a condition that sometimes resulted when officers were left too long in a particular environment. Some thought that this particular restriction on the employment of officers was extremely short-sighted. After all, the MAAG community needed officers with deep talents. By prohibiting repetitive tours to the same country of the same linguistic region, the Army was forfeiting many operational advantages.[24]

Availability was another inhibitor of matching officer skills with positions. Again, this problem was particularly evident in the case of MAAG assignments, where continuity of effort was considered absolutely essential. In the MAAG community, personnel underlap was to be avoided at all costs. To have an advisor on station by his predecessor's departure date, it was often necessary for the Army to waive the special qualifications for the position in question and for the selected officer to forego the extensive training that was supposed to precede such an assignment. Despite the fact that scores of officers might possess the background and skills necessary to excel in a particular position, considerations of availability often dictated that marginally qualified officers would fill the slot.[25]

Assigning the best officer to a particular job was often thwarted by local commanders, who, by exercising their broad assignment prerogatives, looked after their own staffing needs first and placed incoming officers where they were most needed. All too often, the skills and qualifications of the officer affected were only a secondary consideration. Many officers found themselves performing roles for which they were neither requisitioned nor trained.

The Army's ability to align officer qualifications with particular jobs was further reduced by the relatively primitive methods used to categorize both officers and duty positions. Officer skills were vaguely defined. Only branch, grade, and MOS were normally used in officer requisitions. Descriptions of duty positions were equally as ambiguous. They were, as a general rule, not crafted in terms of experience or skills but in the broad and imprecise language used to categorize officer qualifications. Consequently, officers with unclear skills were assigned to duties with vague or incomplete job descriptions. Thus, when the right officer was employed in the right position, it often occurred by accident.[26]

The Army's senior leaders contemplated taking action that would permit personnel managers to find better matches between skills and positions. Some saw the problem in terms of restricted avenues for promotion success for officers with specialized knowledge or talents. Only by widening the pathways to the ranks of senior leadership, they believed, could the Army hope to retain those individuals with deep talents. To remedy what it saw as an officer employment crisis, the Haines Board, in 1966, recommended that those officers who had developed "expertise in depth" be allowed to advance to the highest ranks of the Army without commanding at the battalion level and above.[27]

The recommendation of the Haines Board was not, as one can imagine, received with universal acclaim by the Officer Corps. Many senior officers, while conceding that it was necessary to nurture special talent, were not prepared to go so far as to reward experts with high rank. Experts were to be given a separate and less prestigious career track than the more successful generalists who bore greater responsibilities, possessed greater potential, and had endured the tough assignments. Officers with deep talents were, to paraphrase a popular slogan of the day, to be kept on tap and not on top.[28]

THE 1970s AND EARLY-1980s

In the 1970s, the Army introduced a new officer career management model after recognizing that it was developing too many jacks of all trades and far too few experts. The Officer Personnel Management System (OPMS), the name given to the new career progression paradigm, was designed, among other things, to rectify this and produce officers with the deep talents necessary to address the many tasks that the Army was being asked to perform.

The idea behind OPMS was to match the skills, aptitudes, and experience of officers with appropriate duty positions—placing the right people in the right jobs. The system operated under the dual track concept, which entailed the requirement for every officer to acquire proficiency in a primary and secondary skill area. Officers had to identify their primary and secondary skill areas prior to promotion to major and achieve proficiency in these areas prior to their promotion to lieutenant colonel. Normally, an officer's primary skill was his basic branch while his secondary skill was in either a functional area or in one of the special career programs.[29]

Even before it was put into effect, many officers expressed deep reservations about OPMS. General Creighton Abrams, the Army Chief of Staff at the time, had several concerns, including: that OPMS, by emphasizing specialization, would compartmental-ize, fragment, and undermine the unity of the Officer Corps; that it would become so rigid and so inflexible that it would force each officer into a narrow mold, thereby making it more difficult to develop officers who were willing to perform the tough, unstructured jobs in operational units; that the system would be so complex that it would be unmanageable; and that OPMS would subordinate the broad interests of the Army to narrow special interests.[30]

The upshot was that, despite the recognition that the Army had to do a better job matching up officer skills with duty positions, there was very little change in the way the Army employed its officers. Once again, the Army found that the generalist proclivities of the vast majority of combat arms officers were so in-grained that they could not be dislodged. Competitive officers knew that specialization was to be avoided at all costs, and the quickest and surest route to the top remained the frequent rotation through a variety of assignments.

The assignment process during this period was constrained by the same type of considerations that had constrained it in the past. These considerations worked against both the implementation of OPMS and the broader goal of assigning the right officer to the right position. Just as there had been in the past, there was a concerted push throughout the 1970s and early-1980s to ensure that each organization received its fair share of high quality officers. The DCSPER attempted to distribute the top, middle, and bottom third of the

Officer Corps evenly among units. All organizations and all commanders should, the idea was, operate from roughly the same quality baseline. Moreover, personnel managers were instructed to distribute former battalion commanders as well as graduates of the Command and General Staff College (CGSC) and the USAWC evenly across the Army. Many of these top performers were placed in jobs for which they had no background, of course, but that did not matter to the receiving organizations, whose leaders were more focused on attitude and general background that on skills. The prevailing assumption about the employment of officers remained that all good officers should be able to handle almost any job.[31]

Throughout most of the 1970s and into the early-1980s, budget cuts and stabilization constraints made the task of matching duty positions with expertise more difficult. To maintain continuity, improve unit performance, and save money, officers were frozen in certain assignments for extended periods of time. This affected their availability. Prescribed command tour lengths, lieutenant colonel and colonel command selection and programming, and, as always, assignment "equity" (i.e., the idea that everyone should share equally in short tours, hardship tours, family separations, etc.) further constricted assignment windows. These factors and others made it extremely difficult for personnel managers to place the right officer in the right spot.[32]

CONCLUSIONS

Throughout the 20th century, the U.S. Army embraced a career progression model originally intended to develop broadly experienced generalists capable of leading a vast citizen Army in the event of a national emergency. The employment formula intrinsic to this model entailed a frequent rotation of duty among a wide variety of assignments at progressively higher levels. The model rested on the assumptions that: a good officer could do almost any job well; specialization or repetitive assignments in one field was antithetical to leader development; and only those officers who had endured the tough and unstructured jobs in operational units should be rewarded with high rank.

While the officer employment practices inherent in this career progression model made a great deal of sense in the interwar period, they became increasingly misaligned with actual Army needs as the century progressed. Technological progress, the changing nature of war, the increasing complexity of the military profession, the expanding list of Army missions, and the gradual economic and social transformation of the nation created a greater demand for officers with deep talents and specialized knowledge. This was evidenced by the steeply and continuously rising percentage of officers who were assigned to nonoperational slots after World War II. Despite these developments, the career progression paradigm articulated to produce generalists capable of leading an industrial age Army demonstrated a remarkable resilience and maintained a powerful hold on the collective conscience of the Officer Corps.

This is not to say that the Army was oblivious to the need to create highly skilled specialists to meet the demands of an increasingly sophisticated defense establishment. In fact, even during the interwar period, attention was given to aligning officer skills with duty positions. But recognition of this need did not translate into effective action.

There were a number of long-standing policies, practices, and considerations, some of which were outgrowths of the career progression model itself, which inhibited changes in employment practices. Considerations involving fairness of assignment or "equity of duty," budgetary restrictions, officer availability, and legislative requirements often worked against matching officer skills with Army needs. So, too, did the Army's very general and vague methods of categorizing officer qualifications. These methods worked fine in a system designed to produce broadly experienced generalists but were unequal to the task of identifying and employing specialized talent.

ENDNOTES - CHAPTER 6

1. Committee No. 8, "Promotion, Separation and Assignment of Regular Army Officer in Time of Peace: Modification to Develop an Efficient and Well Balanced Officer Personnel System," Conference Report, G-1, Carlisle, PA: USAWC Curricular Files, October 25, 1933, p. 3.

2. Richard Harry Yarger, *Army Officer Personnel Management: The Creation of the Modern American System to 1939*, Ph.D. Dissertation, Philadelphia, PA: Temple University, January 1996, pp. 341-344.

3. *Ibid.*, pp. 444-448, 460, 470-477, 493-496.

4. John W. Masland and Laurence I. Radway, *Soldiers and Scholars: Military Education and National Policy*, Princeton, NJ: Princeton University Press, 1957, p. 20.

5. George R. Iverson, *Officer Personnel Management: A Historical Perspective*, Carlisle, PA: U.S. Army War College, May 1978, p. 17.

6. As quoted in George W. Putnam, Jr., *Generalization versus Specialization in the US Army Officer Corps*, Carlisle, PA: U.S. Army War College, June 1960, p. 3.

7. *DA Pamphlet 600-3, Career Planning for Army Officers*, Washington, DC: Department of the Army, 1956, p. 7.

8. As quoted in Putnam, p. 3.

9. James R. Johnson, *Balanced Officer Programs, Individual Study*, Carlisle, PA: U.S. Army War College, March 1959, p. 13.

10. Kenneth L. Johnson, *Qualitative Distribution of Officer Personnel*, Carlisle, PA: U.S. Army War College, March 1959, pp. 20, 31.

11. Putnam, p. 24.

12. Houck Spencer, *Evaluation of the Regular Officer Corps of the United States Army by Historical Professional Standards*, Carlisle, PA: U.S. Army War College, March 1958, pp. 20-21.

13. Charles J. Denholm, *Officer Promotion and Elimination*, Carlisle, PA: U.S. Army War College, March 1956, p. 9.

14. Clarence W. Drye, *Responsibility Pay for Officers*, Carlisle, PA: U.S. Army War College, January 1960, p. 4.

15. *Ibid.*, p. 22.

16. Edward Bautz, Jr., *Imponderables of Officer Personnel Management*, Carlisle, PA: U.S. Army War College, March 1958, p. 43.

17. Robert H. Nevins, Jr., *The Retention of Quality Junior Officers – A Challenge for the Seventies*, Carlisle, PA: U.S. Army War College, March 1970, p. 42.

18. Willard Latham, *The Army as a Career*, Carlisle, PA: U.S. Army War College, February 1968, p. 28.

19. Walter F. Ulmer, *Concepts of Generalization and Specialization in Officer Career Management*, Carlisle, PA: U.S. Army War College, March 1969, p. 38.

20. Latham, p. 28.

21. Thaddeus Holt, *The Army Officer Corps and the Pentagon in 1965-1967: Miscellaneous Observations*, Vol. 7, Thaddeus Holt Papers. 1 Box, Carlisle, PA: Archives of the U.S. Army Heritage and Education Center, p. 10.

22. Putnam, p. 25.

23. Kay Wieland, *Junior Officer Retention: The Army's Dilemma*, Carlisle, PA: U.S. Army War College, March 1970, p. 18.

24. Alvin D. Ungerleider, *Missionaries for the Whole World: Senior Army Officer Selection and Education for Assignments to Developing Areas*, Carlisle, PA: U.S. Army War College, March 1967, p. 18.

25. Frank A. LaBoon, *Senior Army Officer Selection and Education for Assignments to Developing Areas*, Carlisle, PA: U.S. Army War College, March 1967, p. 9.

26. Ulmer, p. 56.

27. Department of the Army, *Report of the Department of the Army Board to Review Army Officer Schools*, Haines Board, Washington, DC: February 1966, p. I:32.

28. Holt, p. 15.

29. Iverson, p. 58.

30. *Ibid.*, p. 72.

31. *Ibid.*, p. 74.

32. *Ibid.*

CHAPTER 7

EVALUATING OFFICER TALENT

INTRODUCTION

The principal purpose of the Officer Evaluation Report (OER), or officer efficiency report as it was known until 1973, has been to serve as a basis for personnel decisions. Matters of promotion, elimination, retention in grade, command selection, and school selection have all rested heavily on the strength of a given officer's evaluation. Furnishing personnel managers with information necessary for the proper assignment and utilization of officers has been another aim of these reports. More recently, the OER has been employed as a tool for professional development. Over the last several decades, evaluation reports have attempted to stimulate an active interchange between superiors and subordinates, giving the latter the opportunity to benefit from the former's knowledge and experience and ensuring that the rated officer was fully aware of his superior's expectations.

Unfortunately, the OER has not, in the main, lived up to the exalted hopes that the Army and its leaders have had for it. It has been bedeviled by a host of internal and seemingly intractable flaws that make it of marginal value both to the Department of the Army (DA) and to the individual officer. This chapter will sketch the evolution of the OER and offer some thoughts about the reasons behind its inadequacy.

HISTORICAL OVERVIEW

From the inception of the Army until World War I, officer evaluation reports varied widely—from the rather desultory and unstructured narratives intermittently rendered by commanders of the Continental Army during the Revolution to the highly complex 24-page annual reports used on the eve of World War I. The former often told practically nothing about the rated officer while the latter normally provided an overabundance of detail. Throughout most of the 19th century, the Army relied principally upon two types of evaluations to gauge the effectiveness of its officers—letter reports to the Secretary of War or the Adjutant General and the written assessments provided by the Inspector General. Both types of report aided in the selection of officers for permanent commissions and in the weeding out of less effective officers in the aftermath of conflicts. They proved to be especially useful in this latter role following the War of 1812 when, faced with drastic budget cuts, the Army had to trim its bloated Officer Corps down to a size that it could afford. To effect the desired reductions, the Secretary of War issued a general order directing that efficiency reports be submitted on all officers. It required that the reporting officers rank their subordinates as "Outstanding," "Of the Second Order of Merit," or "Average." With these reports, it was hoped, rational choices could be made about which officers would be retained and which officers would be encouraged to return to their civilian careers.[1]

Beginning in the early-1880s, the evaluation of officers became a matter of much concern in the War Department. This concern, stimulated by a newfound professionalism growing out of industrialization, eventually led to the introduction of an experimental two-part report in 1890. In the first section of this report, the officer was required to write a self-evaluation. In the second section, the rater provided an assessment of the rated officer's ability and proficiency. This report was in use Army-wide by 1895. In 1904, a new four-page evaluation form was introduced. Over the next decade, this form was subjected to almost constant scrutiny and underwent numerous revisions. The trend was toward more detailed and lengthy reports. By 1911, the report had expanded to 11 pages; by 1912, to 20 pages; and in 1914, to 24 pages. Complaints about the length and complexity of the evaluation resulted in the report being reduced to 12 pages by 1917, on the eve of America's entrance into World War I.[2]

In 1922, a rating form was developed that used a graphic rating scale to assess the qualifications and achievements of officers. The form consisted of a series of qualification and achievement scales on which an officer was rated on five scales of efficiency. These were adjectival ratings ranging from "unsatisfactory" to "superior." Written comments by the rater and endorser, describing in their own words the officer's performance on the job, were included in the report. Later, during the interwar period, a numerical score was introduced. These scores were averaged and the numerical average was interpreted in terms of one of the five adjectival equivalents.[3]

Rating inflation set in almost immediately after the report was introduced. This trend resulted in a steady decline in the validity of this evaluation instrument. A possible reason behind this inflation was the establishment of minimum efficiency rating standards for assignment to certain service schools. Many raters marked their reports in terms of what they wanted to happen to their subordinates rather than the rating that the officers actually deserved.

The interwar OER was generally well received by officers because, as it turned out, everyone soon received an "excellent" rating or above. The relative significance of a given numerical score fell lower, with the downward trend in rating standards. By 1938, only about 5 percent of the Officer Corps was receiving a "below excellent" rating. The DA could not depend upon OER scores to distinguish truly superior officers from their fellows. A colonel could be rated "superior," the highest rating possible, and still be below average for his grade. A captain could be rated as "excellent," and still be exceeded by 95 percent of all captains. No one could tell where a given "superior" or "excellent" officer stood.[4]

The rating form introduced in 1922, with relatively slight modifications, became Form 67 in 1936. Form 67 remained in use until 1947, when it was superseded by Form 67-1. The adoption of the latter form emerged from a program of scientific research conducted at the end of World War II. This research compared the relative merits of several different efficiency reporting systems with the object of selecting the best. Thousands of officers representing all branches, grades, components, and echelons took part in this effort. Form 67-1 emerged from this project and was adopted for official use in July 1947.[5]

The new report introduced three fairly radical innovations in efficiency reporting. First, Form 67-1 was "validated." This meant that, for the first time, an OER was tried out before its adoption to determine if the rating accomplished by the form was related to some other measure of officer efficiency. The second innovation was concerned with the manner in which the results of the rating were expressed — the type of score. A decision was reached to employ the Army Standard Rating, which was a relative-score scale permitting comparisons among officers. A third, and by far the most controversial innovation, concerned the actual content of the form. A new type of item was used, the so-called forced-choice item.

The new form was extremely unpopular. For one thing, it did not require the rater to show the report to the rated officer. It was hoped that the secretive nature of the report would reduce rating inflation. From the perspective of personnel managers, this made perfect sense. Army leaders considered the report an evaluative and not a developmental tool; i.e., as a tool for use in personnel actions rather than as a source of information for the officer. There was consequently no practical need to share the information with the person being rated.[6]

The most common complaint against the new OER, however, was that it did allow the rater to determine the numerical rating he gave to a subordinate. The forced distribution scheme resulted in clear cut winners and losers. This was by design. The Army believed it could eliminate or substantially reduce inflation by obscuring the numerical scores and by forcing raters to make real and oftentimes painful distinctions.

Soon after it was fielded, raters began to subvert the system by attempting to outguess the values assigned by the DA to their evaluations. Change soon became necessary, and a new version of the evaluation report was introduced in 1950 (DA Form 67-2). The Army had commenced work on the new OER before hostilities broke out in Korea. At that time, preliminary rating content had been developed and full-scale validity research was in preparation. But the demands of the Korean crisis necessitated a cancellation of these research studies. Advantage was taken of progress already made in developing rating scales for the new OER, and these scales were incorporated directly into Form 67-2. This form was introduced in September 1950, with scoring weights determined administratively — a decision made necessary by the Korean emergency.[7]

The new Form 67-2 consisted of five sections. Section I contained information to identify the rated officer and the endorser, and space for the written comments of those individuals. No score was attached to the comments, but these remarks did prove helpful in distinguishing between officers. Sections II, III, and IV contained the scored scales: Section II covered "Estimated Desirability in Various Capacities" and was similar to a section on the old Form 67-1. Section II and IV contained new rating scales. Research had indicated that there was a limit to the number of scales on which a rater could make useful distinctions. Two scales that raters could distinguish were "performance on present assignments" and "promotability," so these scales were included in Section III. A scale of "overall value to the Army" (Section IV) was adopted because it permitted the rater to combine into one single evaluation all of the ratings on specific aspects. Like its predecessor, however, Form DA 67-2 enjoyed only a short existence. It was replaced in 1953 by DA Form 67-3, which was, in turn, superseded by Form DA 67-4 in 1956. In each case, the inflation of ratings proved to be a major problem.[8]

In 1951, the Army adopted the Officer Efficiency Index (OEI) as a tool for managing officers. While Form DA 67-2 was being developed, research on the basic problems associated with efficiency reporting had been pursued energetically. One major finding was that no particular type of rating technique reduced differences among raters as much as did averaging a number of reports, regardless of the type of rating technique used. This finding pointed to the need for developing an averaging technique as an immediate means of improving the OER system.

The application of an averaging technique to efficiency reports was not new. In the interwar period, the Army used a General Efficiency Rating (GER), which was essentially a 10-year average of OER scores. Various changes were effected to make this index administratively feasible for the much larger early-Cold War Army, one of which was a reduction of the time considered to 5 years. This reduction was intended to strike a balance between increasing the number of available reports for averaging on a given officer and yet having the new index reflect the officer's current status and capabilities rather than his performance in the relatively remote past.

Scores on the OEI introduced in 1951 ranged from 50 to 150 and were based on the Army standard rating scale. The middle officer on Active Duty was assigned an OEI of 100. The symmetrical grouping of scores around the middle were such that approximately two-thirds fell between 80 and 120, about one-sixth above 120, and the remaining one-sixth below 80. The index was considered very valuable in an evaluation system based on industrial age management precepts. It provided a crude but useful gauge of "quality" by which officers could be quickly sorted and categorized as to their role in a future emergency. Personnel managers lamented the Army's decision in 1961 to phase out the OEI since it made their jobs much more laborious.[9]

In the same year that it did away with the OEI, it adopted a new OER, DA Form 67-5. This new form was retained until 1968, when it was replaced by DA Form 67-6, which was superseded by DA Form 67-7 in 1973. In each instance, inflation was a principal reason for the form's replacement. DA Form 67-7 was something of a milestone because, with the adoption of this report, the Army started using the term "officer evaluation report" as opposed to "efficiency report" — a term that had been used for 50 years.[10]

The Form 67-7 remained in effect for 7 years. In 1980, it was replaced with DA Form 67-8. The old report was jettisoned because it did not support the new Officer Personnel Management System (OPMS); it did not encourage the professional development of officers; it did not improve organizational effectiveness; and it became so inflated that it was practically useless as an assessment tool. Form 67-8 integrated several new features that were absent in its predecessor: namely, participation by the rated officer; an enhanced role for the reviewer; an alignment with the OPMS; and a format that was ostensibly more conducive to board and personnel management use. It survived for 17 years, a modern longevity record.[11]

DA Form 67-9 succeeded Form 67-8 in 1997. The new OER was designed, *inter alia*, to make finer distinctions in officer quality, improve the process of senior leader selection, and emphasize junior officer leader development. The developers of the new form purposed to expedite the rapid and even assimilation of junior officers into the Army culture by stimulating greater superior/subordinate communication. To promote this end, they inserted into the new OER a separate junior officer worksheet that required the assignment of developmental tasks for lieutenants based on the Army's leadership doctrine and the unit's mission. An innovative feature of the new rating scheme was its masking of second lieutenant OERs. When these officers would later go before the Major's Board for promotion, only their OERs as first lieutenants and captains would be visible. This feature was added to "level the playing field" since there were, among junior officers, great variations in assignments, experiences, and the rate of assimilation into the Army culture during the early years of their career.[12]

One of the most controversial aspects of the Form 67-9 system was its strict limitation on the number of "Above Center of Mass (ACOM)" ratings that officers could give to their subordinates. Senior raters could bestow ACOM ratings on less than 50 percent of OERs in their profile for each grade. If senior raters exceeded that limitation, their profiles would be invalidated and the rated officers would receive a "Center of Mass (COM)," regardless of the rating contained on the OER. The inflexibility of the system made some senior officers long for times past when the old "Himalayas" system (so named because of the rater profiles many senior leaders acquired under it) allowed more room for the exercise of discretion.[13]

CHALLENGES WITH THE OER

Over the years, there have been many problems with the OER from the perspective of both individual officers and personnel managers. There is not sufficient space in this chapter to list them, let alone discuss them. Consequently, only the most intractable and enduring shortcomings in the evaluation system will be touched upon here.

As indicated previously in this narrative, the most persistent and troublesome of these shortcomings has been inflation; all other deficiencies have paled in comparison. Periods of evaluative equanimity have been infrequent and short-lived. One such episode occurred in the immediate aftermath of World War I. In 1922, for example, three-quarters of all captains received ratings of less than excellent; only about one in 20 earned the top rating of superior; and slightly more than one in five attained an excellent rating. This breakout resulted in a typical Gaussian curve. Subsequent years, however, witnessed a progressive inflation of the reports until by 1945, 99 percent of officers received one of the top two ratings.[14]

This inflation, in fact, prevented General George C. Marshall, the Army's Chief of Staff, from relying on efficiency reports to select general officers at the outbreak of World War II. The expansion of the Army that began in 1940 created a need for 150 additional general officers. Of the 4,000 officers eligible by grade and experience to be promoted to that august rank, 2,000 were, on the basis of their evaluation reports, found to be superior and suited for this honor. The outstanding officer could not be distinguished from the good. As a result, Marshall and selection boards had to depend on their own judgment and personal knowledge of the officers being considered to make their decisions.[15]

This trend of inordinately high ratings continued in subsequent decades. DA Forms 67-1 through 67-8 all experienced significant inflation within a short time of their introduction. In some cases, it was a matter of a few months. It took about 90 days, for example, for the DA to determine that raters and endorsers using DA Form 67-6 (adopted for Army wide use in March 1968) were giving "higher than warranted" evaluations to subordinates. The new form soon became as useless as its predecessor in guiding promotion and selection boards in their choices. These boards, like the ones convened by Marshall at the beginning of World War II, found themselves relying principally on their own judgments for their selections.[16]

One frustrated and cynical War College student summed up the history of OER inflation as follows:

> The adoption of a new report may lower the inflation-ary trend for a short time, as happened in the past; however, as has also happened with every report since [the early 1920s], inflation will take over, making the new report as useless for use by selection boards as the previous ones.[17]

Another common criticism of the OER system is that it has not attached sufficient weight to potential or to long-term professional development. Tradition-ally, the evaluation report has focused on current performance and short-term results. Thus, the impor-tance of outcomes that are long-term and qualitative in nature tend to be minimized while the significance of accomplishments that render immediate and easily measured results have usually been over-emphasized. This myopic approach to officer evaluation has several consequences. First, it stifles innovation by rewarding those who follow established paths and accept con-ventional wisdom. Second, it favors those who excel at organizational and direct types of leadership while overlooking those with strategic leadership abilities.[18]

A lack of comprehensiveness and specificity has been another long-standing complaint about the eval-uation system. Reports have not recorded or identified the specific skills, knowledge, and talents developed or exhibited by officers while serving in particular positions. They have consequently been of limited value to personnel managers in finding officers with particular talents for particular jobs. The "company man" developmental model that informs the Army's officer management system has been responsible for this, or at least much of it. In this model, positions are usually not sufficiently defined to allow for precise evaluation. The Army has looked for people that can handle the mass of "tough, unstructured" jobs that predominate within operational units — not for specialists with particular talents.[19]

Many observers have commented on the general lack of confidence displayed by officers toward the evaluation system. This lack of confidence is largely a function of the sharp and dramatic variances in rating behavior that flow from the many complex pressures and influences that make up the rating environment and which, many are convinced, have distorted the evaluation system. Over the years, many officers have felt that their professional fate depended too heavily on the writing ability of their superiors. As they saw it, it was not so much what they did but how effective their rater or reviewer was in describing what they did. Frequent changes in rating scales, procedures, and forms have also lessened the validity of the OER in the minds of countless officers. Not only has the basic form changed, on average, every 7 years, but there have been frequent changes to each form over its administrative lifetime. In its first 10 months in use, for example, Form 67-6 had eight major modifications made to it.[20]

The OER scoring system itself has been a target of almost constant criticism. As we have seen, because raters generally have seen the OER as unfair, they have resorted to "scheming" to protect their subordinates and register a subtle protest against the system. In the late-1940s, raters tried to "outguess" the values assigned by the DA to OERs, making the evaluation system into a type of game. Presently, reviewers parcel out their COM and ACOMS in such a way so as to ensure that all deserving officers have a "heartbeat." In both cases, performance and potential were often secondary considerations. The scaling instruments that have provided the "quantitative" part of the OER have been denounced by many observers as "utterly inappropriate" and "manifestly unfair." These instruments have been suitable for measuring comparable performances such as those measured on academic tests. When applied to OERs, however, where the duties and responsibilities of even ostensibly similar positions vary widely, they have very limited assessment value.[21]

CONCLUSION

The officer evaluation system has had a tortuous and troubled history in the U.S. Army. Its tendency toward inflation, its inability to distinguish performance from potential, its inadequacy as a professional development tool, its lack of precision and specificity, its myopic focus, its scaling problems, and its failure to inspire confidence in those whose fate it regulates has prevented the OER, in the various forms it has assumed over the years, from fulfilling the purposes for which it was allegedly designed. Already quite noticeable during the industrial age, these deficiencies and shortcomings have become even more pronounced and visible after the advent of the information age. To be sure, many officers with exceptional direct and organizational skills have emerged over the course of the last century despite the failings in the evaluation system. Whether or not this system will aid in the development of the kind of strategic thinkers that many observers are convinced will be necessary to deal with the multifarious challenges of the future is another question.

ENDNOTES - CHAPTER 7

1. Marlin Craig, *History of the Officer Efficiency Report System, United States Army 1775-1917*, Washington, DC: Office of the Chief of Military History, 1953, pp. II-2, II-6, II-17/18; Lieutenant Colonel Carroll B. Hodges, Chief, Personnel Research Branch, Personnel Retrieval and Processing (PR&P) Division, the Adjutant General Staff (TAGO), "The Officer Efficiency Reporting System," 1954, p. 2.

2. Craig, pp. II-2 - III-27; "Subject: Officer Efficiency Reports," *Lesson Plan*, Ft. Jackson, SC: The Adjutant General's School, April 3, 1954.

3. *Ibid.*

4. *Ibid.*

5. David J. Chesler, "The Army Officer Efficiency Reporting System," Transcript of Briefing at Arlington Hall Station, Virginia, December 18, 1953, Washington, DC: Department of the Army, The Adjutant General's Office, Personnel Research Branch, 1953, p. 2.

6. *Ibid.*

7. *Ibid.*

8. Paul S. Williams, *An Evaluation of the US Army Officer Efficiency Reporting System*, Carlisle, PA: U.S. Army War College, March, 1969, p. 4; Sanders A. Cortner, *The Officer Efficiency Report Can Be an Effective Tool for Personnel Management*, Carlisle, PA: U.S. Army War College, February, 1972, pp. 2-3.

9. Cortner, p. 17.

10. *Ibid.*, p. 3; William R. Mattox, *Management by Objective and the New Officer Efficiency Report: A Valid Concept for the Army Reserve*, Carlisle, PA: U.S. Army War College, December 1975, pp. 5-6; James M. Hardaway, *Strategic Leader Development for a 21st Century Army*, Ft. Leavenworth, KS: Command and General Staff College, School of Advanced Studies, p. 2.

11. Charles R. Hamilton, *The Effects of Multiple Constraints on the Army's New Officer Evaluation Report*, Master of Military Studies, Quantico, VA: Marine Corps Command and Staff College, Academic Year 2001-02, p. 7.

12. *Department of the Army Pamphlet No. 623-105, The Officer Evaluation Reporting System "In Brief,"* Washington, DC: Department of the Army, October 1997, pp. 4-7; Hamilton, p. 8.

13. *Ibid.*, p. 13.

14. Charles D. Herron, "Efficiency Reports," *Infantry Journal*, April 1944, pp. 30-32. Robert L. Dilworth, *Efficiency Report Inflation: A Comparative Analysis of U.S. Army and Selected Foreign Military Officer Evaluation Systems*, Masters Thesis, Ft. Leavenworth, KS: U.S. Army Command and Staff College, 1971, p. 2.

15. Herron, p. 32.

16. Williams, p. 22; Cortner, p. 10.

17. Cortner, p. 11.

18. Williams, p. 4; Hardaway, pp. 28-30, 34.

19. Raymond H. Tiffany, *The Officer Efficiency Report System*, Carlisle, PA: U.S. Army War College, March 1956, p. ii; Mattox, pp. 5-6; Hardaway, p. 12.

20. Mattox, pp. 1-2; Williams, pp. 4, 26.

21. Tiffany, pp. ii, 29; Hamilton, pp. 10-14.